INSURANCE LE

ENGLISH LAW FOR

by

PAUL H SHERRIFF

LONDON
WITHERBY & CO. LTD
32-36 Aylesbury Street
London EC1R 0ET
Telephone No. 01-251 5341
Fax No. 01-251 1296

1st Edition 1984

2nd Edition 1987

3rd Edition 1989

MONUMENT SERIES

WITHERBY & CO. LTD.

1989

ISBN 0 948691 86 7

Printed in Great Britain by
Witherby & Co. Ltd.
London

CONTENTS

INTRODUCTION

"Insurance Learners" are a valuable aid to the study of the Qualifying Examination of the Chartered Insurance Institute.

Students in other fields of professional study (banking, accountancy etc.) have at their disposal, in addition to main texts, "slim volumes" which, ideally, serve both as preliminary **reading** and **revision** texts. Insurance Learners aim to fulfil a similar function for CII students. **The Learner will help the student to organise his thoughts and gain insight into the study material before moving on to the main text** which should be studied more effectively as a result. Once the study of the main text has been completed it is suggested that frequent revision should be undertaken with the aid of the Learner, the presentation of which is designed to facilitate such an approach. The publishers recommend that Learners are most effectively used when the main text is that which has been published by the CII Tuition Service to fulfil the requirements of the same syllabus.

In this Learner questions from previous examination papers are set out, by kind permission of the Chartered Insurance Institute. Questions are grouped according to topic areas but some questions, of course, ask the student to bring in aspects of a number of topics. The student is advised to draw up framework answers to ALL questions and convert as many as possible to fully written solutions.

Examiners in this subject report with a dismaying regularity that inadequate examination technique and lack of practice in written work are prime causes of failure. These are entirely avoidable shortcomings and it is above all the desire of INSURANCE LEARNING SYSTEMS to encourage a systematic approach to study along with the development of sound examination technique.

How the "Learner" should be used'

The "Learner" is more than just a crammer — rather it is a succinct complement to a planned programme of study and a valuable revision aid. You should:

1) Locate the topic to be studied in the "Learner" and read it.
2) Read the topic as covered by the main CII textbook and as directed by the lecturer if attending a class.

   Note taking from the main text, and during oral tuition should be easier and more effective now that the "Learner" has opened up the topic area.
3) Re-read the topic in the "Learner", revising frequently from your notes and the Learner.
4) Attempt "framework" answers to ALL questions coverting as many as possible into full solutions. Discuss your work with others.

I should like finally to express my gratitude to my friends to whom this modest book is dedicated. I am particularly grateful to Carol Bennett for his invaluable advice, support and assistance as well as to Teresa for her unswaying encouragement and help throughout. I also wish to record my thanks to Pat and Janet for contributing to typing the manuscript and to Heather Harris for her valuable contribution to the text.

March 1989
P.H.S.

THE SYLLABUS

AREAS OF STUDY

On completion of this subject the student should:

(a) *be aware of* the sources of English law, namely custom, common law, equity, statute law, case law, judicial precedent;
(b) *be aware of* the differences between civil and criminal law;
(c) *be aware of* the administrative structure of English Law;
(d) *be aware of* the various classes of legal person, namely natural persons, corporations, unincorporated associations and partnerships, the Crown;
(e) *understand* the principal features of the law of contract, namely the essential elements of a valid contract, privity of contract, fraud and misrepresentation, conditions and warranties, illegal and unenforceable contracts, assignments of rights and liabilities, discharge of contract and remedies for breach of contract, law of agency;
(f) *understand* the principal features of the law of tort, namely the nature of tortious liability, general defences to actions in tort, capacity, joint torts, vicarious liability, survival of actions, remedies in the law of tort, limitation.

(Reproduced by kind permission of the Chartered Insurance Institute).

ABOUT THE AUTHOR

Paul Sherriff read Economics at the University College of Wales, Aberystwyth. He subsequently went into legal practice and qualified as a Solicitor. He has over ten years experience of full time teaching in Colleges of further and higher education and of legal practice with his own firm and as a consultant and locum Solicitor in London. He has experience as an examiner in legal subjects for various professional bodies. Paul enjoys cricket, photography and bird watching.

THE CHARTERED INSURANCE INSTITUTE

INTRODUCTORY, QUALIFYING AND L.A.S.C. EXAMINATIONS

APRIL 1989

SUBJECT 020

ENGLISH LAW

Three hours are allowed for this paper. Answer SIX questions only. All questions carry equal marks.

---

1 (a) Distinguish between libel and slander.

(b) Robert has written a humorous article, published in a local newspaper, concerning the activities of a negligent doctor named Doctor Foster. Robert thought this name to be fictitious, but there is a doctor of this name practising locally and this doctor intends suing the newspaper for defamation.

Advise the newspaper.

2. (a) John offers, in January, to sell Paul a bicycle. Paul makes no communication to John until May that year, when he accepts.

Is the offer still open for acceptance? Give reasons.

(b) Janet writes to Vicky "I will sell you my horse for £1,000. If I hear nothing from you before next Saturday, I will take it that you have accepted." Vicky does not reply by Saturday.

Is Vicky legally bound to buy the horse? Give reasons.

3. (a) State the exceptions to the rule that subsequent impossibility of frustration is no defence to an action for breach of contract.

(b) Hatton Garden Limited manufacturers expensive jewellery in England and imports diamonds from Gemstones in Ruritania. Hatton Garden Limited recently placed an order for £500,000 worth of diamonds from Gemstones and paid a deposit of £50,000. The contract is governed by English law. Civil war has now broken out in Ruritania and the Ruritanian government refuses to allow the export of diamonds.

State, giving reasons, whether Hatton Garden Limited can recover the deposit of £50,000.

4. Michael is playing golf and hits a ball an unusually long distance. The ball glances off a tree and hits David, another golf player, who loses the sight of an eye. David sues Michael for negligence.

Advise Michael.

5. (a) Who is eligible for jury service?

(b) In which courts are juries used?

(c) What is the composition and function of a jury in a criminal trial?

6. What are the basic rules regarding the operation of precedent in (a) the civil courts and (b) the criminal courts?

7. (a) What is delegated legislation?

(b) What are the advantages and disadvantages of delegated legislation?

8. (a) What is a limited partnership?

(b) What the main effects of the incorporation of a business into a limited liability company?

CHAPTER 1.

SOURCES OF ENGLISH LAW

THE NATURE OF LAW

1.01 The law of a particular state means the body of rules designed to regulate human conduct which is recognised as valid within the state and which is enforced by its officials.

English Law is the body of rules recognised and enforced in England and Wales. Northern Ireland and Scotland have separate legal systems although all three jurisdictions share a final appeal court, namely the House of Lords. The law which is enforced by the courts must be distinguished from what is sometimes referred to as "natural" or "moral" law. In most cases the rules of law and morality clearly coincide but this is by no means inevitable.

The basic aim of law is the attainment of justice in society. When applied to particular circumstances, however, the degree of justice hoped for cannot always be achieved, e.g. the law usually requires that someone is at fault before compensation for injuries can be required.

1.02 The following **characteristics** distinguish the English legal system from those of other countries:

1. **Continuity** — the law has developed continuously over many centuries. A particular law does not become inoperative merely because of the passage of time — e.g. the Treason Act of 1351 was considered in **Joyce -v- D.P.P.** (1946).
2. **Absence of Codification** — In some countries most of the law has been reduced to written code which contain the entire law on a particular subject. Generally this is not so in England and Wales.
3. **The System of Precedent** — (See Later)
4. **The independence of the Judiciary and Legal Profession** — Judges are not subject to control from the government and may, if appropriate, give judgment against the Crown. Lawyers (i.e. Barristers and Solicitors) are not state officials and as a tradition are not influenced by political considerations in their choice of clients.
5. **The concurrent development of systems of common law and equity** — (See later).
6. **The accusatorial or contentious procedure** under which, in both Civil and Criminal cases, the court remains neutral and hears arguments from both sides. This approach is to be contrasted with **inquisitorial** procedure which is far more a feature of continental legal systems.

7. **The absence of Roman law influences** Many legal systems are based upon Roman Law but the English system has been only marginally affected by it.

1.03 THE MAIN SOURCES OF ENGLISH LAW

The meaning of the expression "sources of law".

Usual Meaning — the term usually refers to the means by which the law is brought into existence including legislation, judicial precedent, European law and custom.

Other meanings sometimes attributed to the term "sources of law" are:

The Literary Source i.e. where the law is physically found e.g. law reports, statutes and textbooks.

The Formal Source i.e. the authority gives force to the rules of law in the state.

The Historical Source i.e. the reasons behind the creation of the law such as government white papers or reports by the Law Commission.

Much of our law derives from what are known as the rules of "common law", and "equity", largely embodied in judicial decisions known as "case law", and from Acts of Parliament. There are other specific sources, some very old such as "custom", others very modern, such as the laws emerging as enforceable community rights from the United Kingdom's membership of the European Economic Community.

1.04 COMMON LAW

Traditionally this is the main source of English law. Common law is unwritten law consisting of a body of rules that have grown to be accepted in the course of time and which have been elevated to the status of law through being acknowledged as such by judges in superior courts.

You should refer to the main texts for a detailed historical account of the development of common law and equity, which is beyond the scope of this book.

Much of English law is not in the form of deliberate or express decisions by Parliament. The early judges travelled the country, determining issues and giving reasoned decisions thereon based upon practicality and common sense. In time these judgments were recorded and followed when similar cases arose. In this way cases "common" to the country as a whole developed. The decisions and the precedents they established, made by the superior courts, became binding on the local courts throughout the land.

1.05 EQUITY

Some of the common law rules or their application in particular circumstances were preceived to be arbitary, harsh, and sometimes although lawful, unfair. As a response to this a great body of rules known as "equity" gradually emerged over a period of centuries largely as a result of the various inadequacies or defects in the common law.

The King was petitioned by subjects dissatisfied with the common law and these petitions were passed to the Lord Chancellor (who was invariably a cleric) for him to determine. As an ecclesiastic the Chancellor was more concerned with the principle that persons should comply with their moral obligations than with the strict letter of the law. Eventually this process led to the establishment of the Court of Chancery.

The rules of equity were far more concerned with the **reality** or **substance** of a legal relationship as opposed to the common law which was principally concerned with matters of **form**, e.g. its strict insistence on the proper form of writ being used to commence legal proceedings. To some extent the difference in the approach of common law rules and those of equity continues today. The common law generally provided only one remedy for the successful litigant, namely damages (i.e. financial compensation). This was often inappropriate and equity provided additional and more effective remedies, such as **injunctions, specific performance** and **rescission.** Even today it is true to say that whilst the common law remedy of damages is normally available as of right to the succesful litigant, the equitable remedies are all **discretionary.** In other words the court still considers not merely legalistic rules but also the promptings of fairness and conscience.

The development of equity took place in parallel with that of the common law and the two systems were administered quite independently until 1873. In that year the **administration** of the two systems was fused into one with the result that all courts could award both common law and equitable remedies. The 1873 Judicature Act also provided that in cases where the principles of common law and equity should conflict, equity should prevail. This provision is now contained in the **Supreme Court Act 1981, s.49.**

1.06 STATUTE LAW OR LEGISLATION

Legislation — law making — is undertaken by Parliament and new laws are made by **Acts of Parliament,** otherwise referred to as **statutes.** As a law making body Parliament is supreme in the United Kingdom. In constitutional theory there is nothing which Parliament cannot do by statute.

Statues may therefore amend or abolish established rules of common law or equity; overrule the effects of decisions of the courts: or make entirely new laws on matters which previously have not been the subject of legislation. In the United Kingdom, Parliament consists of three discrete elements: the **Sovereign,** the **House of Lords,** and the **House of Commons.** To become law proposals known as "Bills' must be approved by the House of Commons, House of Lords and receive from the Queen, the Royal Assent. In practice the Royal Assent is a mere formality and, owing to the Parliament Acts of 1911 and 1949, the power of the House of Lords is very much more restricted e.g. it has virtually no influence over "money bills", i.e. proposed legislation which in the opinion of the Speaker of the House of Commons contains provisions dealing with finance and taxation. In other cases the House of Lords has limited powers to delay the progress of legislation and, therefore, real power resides, quite properly, with the elected House of Commons.

1.07 **TYPES OF LEGISLATION**

As previously mentioned proposed legislation is referred to as a ''Bill'' as it passes through the appropriate stages in the Lords and Commons. There are three main types of Bill:-

(a) **Private Members Bill.** A private member may introduce a Bill, although it is most unlikely to be successful in passing through the necessary stages unless it is adopted by the government. The opportunity to present a Private Members Bill is limited owing to the pressure on Parliamentary time and a ballot is held early in the session to decide the order in which members may introduce a Bill.

(b) **Private Bill.** These are Bills for the special interest or benefit of a person or organisation. The most common presenters of these Bills are Local Authorities wishing to widen the scope of their existing powers.

(c) **Public Bills.** These affect the community at large and are usually introduced by the government but occasionally private members initiate them.

1.08 **THE PROCESS OF A STATUTE**

The procedure which follows usually starts in the House of Commons before going to the Lords but the reverse can occur:-

1. **First Reading**
   The Bill is formally presented and there is usually little debate.
2. **Second Reading**
   There is a debate on the general principles of the Bill and, if it is at all opposed, a vote is taken.
3. **Committee Stage**
   This is crucial as the proposed legislation is examined in detail and individual clauses may be amended or even excluded.
4. **Report Stage**
   The House is informed of changes that have been made and may itself make additional amendment.
5. **Third Reading**
   Generally only minor amendments are possible.

Public Bills lapse if they have not completed all the above stages by the time a session of Parliament has been ended by prorogation or when Parliament is dissolved for a general election. It may be reintroduced in another session of Parliament but the Bill must pass through all the stages once again.

1.09 CODIFICATION AND CONSOLIDATION

Codification entails the gathering together of all existing legislation and case law on one topic into one Act e.g. the **Partnership Act 1890** and the **Bills of Exchange Act 1882.**

Consolidation is the process whereby existing legislation on a particular subject is collected together and re-enacted in one statue. This process is increasingly popular and although it does not alter the law it makes it easier for lawyers and lay people to find. The **1979 Sale of Goods Act** is an example of consolidating legislation and other areas of the law which have recently been consolidated include marriage, taxation and employment protection.

An Act comes into force on the day on which it receives the Royal Assent unless some other date is specified in the Act itself. An Act remains in full force and effect unless and until it is specifically requested or amended by subsequent legislation.

Following from the constitutional doctrine of the supremacy of Parliament there is the power of Parliament to legislate with retroactive or retrospective effect. In practice this power is only exercised very sparingly as many consider the practice legally objectionable (perhaps the equivalent of changing the rules as the game progresses!) but there are various examples of retrospective legislation particularly in the field of taxation e.g. in cases of tax avoidance schemes which are declared void with retrospective effect. A further example occurred with the **War Damages Act 1965** when Parliament effectively reversed the decision of the House of Lords in **Burmah Oil Co -v- Lord Advocate** (1965). In this case the highest Court in the land had ordered the British government to pay compensation to the oil company in respect of oil wells destroyed by H.M. Forces in the face of the Japanese advance into Burma in 1942. However, by passing legislation, Parliament deprived the successful plaintiff of the fruits of its action.

1.10 DELEGATED LEGISLATION

In many instances Parliament lays down the framework of the law and then delegates to other persons or bodies the authority to make laws and rules for specific purposes within the Act. The popularity of this form of legislation is increasing each year and, to some extent, is a reaction to Parliament involving itself in more and more complex areas of law. Provided that they are properly made, such regulations have the same legal force as the Act under which they are made.

Delegated legislation is necessary because:-

(a) Parliament does not have sufficient time to consider and debate minor details required for the routine administration of an Act.

(b) In cases of urgency or emergency Parliament may not have the time to deal with the situation or may not actually be in session.

(c) Members of Parliament may well not have the technical expertise or local knowledge to deal with the necessary details, which are delegated to experts.
(d) It provides a large degree of flexibility in that regulations can be amended or revoked from time to time without the necessity for a new Act.

The Power to make Delegated Legislation arises largely out of the following:-
(a) **Orders in Council.** The Government, usually in times of emergency, may be given power to make laws in this way. This requires a meeting of the Privy Council attended by the Queen and the procedure is a formality.
(b) **Ministers of the Crown.** Ministers may be given the power to make Orders under statutes which affect their own departments e.g. the Transport Minister has the power to vary speed limits and the Chancellor of Exchequer may (temporarily at least) alter rates of tax and duties.
(c) **By-laws.** Local Authorities and other public bodies often have delegated to them the power to make laws within the range of their areas of activity.

Delegated Legislation is technically made public by 'statutory instrument' which term also refers to rules and Orders made by Ministers.

Control of Delegated Legislation.
(a) Parliament itself has the right to inspect every statutory instrument and has a select committee to scrutinise any legislation considered likely to be oppressive. Ultimately Parliament may, of course, revoke the delegated power.
(b) The Courts may declare delegated legislation **Ultra Vires** ("beyond the power") and therefore void if it is considered that the delegated legislation has exceeded the scope of the Act under which it was issued.
(c) Sometimes, before delegated legislation may be put into effect, it is necessary to hold a public enquiry so that opinion can be tested.

1.11 INTERPRETATION OF STATUES

The judges do not make new laws, or alter, amend or repeal old laws. Their role is to **interpret** and **apply** existing law to situations put before them. If legislation contains uncertainties or ambiguities of language, then in the guise of interpretation, the courts do have some scope to widen or narrow its application. However, as the House of Lords have emphasised in **Duport Steels -v- Sirs** (1980) if the statute is clear then the courts have no alternative but to give effect to its plain words even if, in their view, this will lead to unfortunate social consequences.

There are various rules which assist the judiciary in the task of interpreting legislation. These include the following:-

(a) **The Interpretation Act 1978**
Many common words and phrases are defined in this Act and will be interpreted accordingly unless the context indicates the contrary. The word "land" for example includes the buildings thereon. This last point was

well illustrated in **Hutton -v- Esher UDC** (1973) where an Act permitted a council to compulsorily purchase "land" to build sewers. The court held that this included the power to purchase and demolish buildings on the land so that the sewer could be constructed.

Many Acts also contain an **interpretation section** which explains the particular meaning of various words used in that legislation.

(b) **The Literal Rule**

This is the primary and favoured rule of interpretation. It provides that a judge should give words their literal, grammatical meaning even if that leads to unforseen and undesirable consequences.

An example of this rule being applied was **Fisher -v- Bell** (1960) where a shopkeeper who displayed a flick-knife in his window was held not to have "offered it for sale". The display, applying the ordinary rules of contract, was merely an "invitation to treat" and not an offer. Even though the existing law was clearly intended to cover such actions it required amending legislation to plug the loophole which this decision created.

(c) **The Golden Rule**

This is a more flexible approach which follows on from the literal rule in that the ordinary meaning of words is accepted unless this would lead to "manifest absurdity or repugnance". In **Re Sigsworth** (1935) the court held that a man who had murdered his mother could not benefit from her estate. Under the **Administration of Estates Act 1925** the ordinary meaning of the word "issue' would obviously have included the son but in these circumstances this would have been repugnant to public policy.

(d) **The Mischief Rule**

This is the most radical judicial approach to statutory interpretation and is sometimes referred to as **the rule in Heydon's Case** (1584). This approach involves the court addressing itself to the question "what was the mischief (or unsatisfactory state of affairs) which Parliament intended the Act to remedy?" The role of the court is then to adopt an appropriate interpretation which advances the remedy and suppresses the 'mischief'. **Smith -v- Hughes** (1960) is a widely quoted example of the application of this rule.

In addition to these established 'rules' there are additional considerations to be noted.

(e) The "Ejusdem generis" rule — i.e. where specific words are followed by general words the latter are regarded as being restricted to things in the same class as the former. See e.g. **Powell -v- Kempton Racecourse** (1899) and **Evans -v- Cross** (1938).

(f) The express mention of one thing implies the exclusion of another. In other words if specific things are mentioned and are not followed by general words, only those specific things are affected by the Act.

(g) "Noscitus a sociis" — i.e. words are interpreted according to their context.

(h) There are certain **presumptions** to which the court should have regard unless they are rebutted by contrary evidence. These include: statutes are not to be of retrospective application; the Crown is not bound by statutes; statutes apply to the whole of the United Kingdom; statutes imposing criminal liability or liability to tax are construed narrowly and in favour of the accused or taxpayer. (See e.g. **Sweet -v- Parsley** (1970).

1.12 EUROPEAN COMMUNITY LAW

This results from the United Kingdom's membership of the European Economic Commission (EEC). The legislation consists of the **Treaties** (the primary legislation) and the **various laws made by European institutions** (the secondary legislation).

(i) **The Treaties**

These automatically became part of our law from 1st January 1973 as a consequence of the European Communities Act 1972.

Rights conferred by the Treaties can be enforced directly in this country and they are not affected by any contrary English legislation see **MacCarthy's Ltd -v- Wendy Smith** (1980).

(ii) **Secondary Legislation**

There are three types of European secondary legislation:-

(a) **Regulations** — Under Article 189 of the EEC Treaty these automatically become part of the law of the Member States the moment they are enacted, e.g. those relating to the tachograph.

(b) **Directives** — These are binding as to the result to be achieved but they leave to the Member States the choice of legislation to achieve that result e.g. the Companies Act 1980 was passed to give effect to the Second Directive on Company Law of the EEC.

(c) **Decisions** — These are binding only on the states or persons to whom they are addressed.

Controls upon EEC Secondary Legislation

(a) If it is ultra vires it can be challenged in the national and European Court.

(b) A special House of Commons Select Committee examines the implications of legislation.

(c) Our representatives in the Council of Ministers can block legislation if it is regarded as contrary to our national interest.

(d) Ultimately Parliament, of course, may repeal the European Communities Act 1972 which rendered the UK subject to European legislation. This is purely theoretical however.

1.13 JUDICIAL PRECEDENT

In their task of resolving disputes in court judges are guided by the previous decisions of other judges in earlier, similar cases.

Judicial precedent is, therefore, the reasoned judgment of a court reached after applying established principles to particular circumstances. This decision then becomes part of the law to be followed by all other inferior courts. If the precedent was created by a higher court to the present one, it is a **binding precedent,** i.e. it must be applied to the present case. If the precedent is not a binding precedent, it may be a **persuasive precedent,** i.e. the court may follow it in the present case, but does not have to do so.

The part of a judgment which is applied in subsequent cases is called the **ratio decidendi.** This should be contrasted with **obiter dicta,** i.e. statements of law made by the judge which are not essential to the decision, e.g. statements made in relation to hypothetical facts used by the judge to illustrate his thinking. Thus in **Castellain -v- Preston** (1883), the judge was dealing with a case involving a fire. His statement that a policy of fire insurance was a contract of indemnity was the ratio decidendi, his statement that a policy of marine insurance was a contract of indemnity was obiter dicta.

The system of judicial precedent can only be understood in relation to the **hierarchy of the courts.** The underlying principle is that the higher courts bind the lower courts. In the civil courts, the system works as follows:-

The House of Lords binds all courts below itself.

The Court of Appeal (Civil Division) binds both itself and the courts below.

The High Court binds the County court but does not bind itself.

The County Court does not create precedents as its decisions are not systematically reported.

In the Criminal Courts, the system works as follows:-

The House of Lords binds all courts below itself.

The Court of Appeal (Criminal Division) binds the courts below, but does not bind itself as the paramount consideration in justice to the individual who stands in peril of losing his liberty.

The Crown Court creates only persuasive precedents.

The Magistrates' Court does not create precedents as its decisions are not systematically reported.

The Judicial Committee of the Privy Council lies outside the English Court system. However, its precedents have strong persuasive force as it is staffed by the Law Lords, i.e. those who staff the House of Lords.

It should be noted that since a statement of the Lord Chancellor in 1966, the House of Lords is no longer bound by its own precedents. It will normally follow them in the interests of certainty, but it will depart from them when the interests of justice demand and allow a proper adaptation of the law to changing social conditions.

It would be wrong to conclude from this account that precedents go without challenge: their authority depends upon the status of the court which created them. The precedents of a lower court can be **reversed** on appeal, e.g. the lower court finds in favour of the plaintiff and the appellate court finds in favour of the defendant; this means, of course, that the earlier precedent is no longer good law. In a later case between different parties before a higher court a precedent can be **overruled:** this does not affect the decision given to the original parties, it merely means that the point of law on which it was made is no longer good law. The facts of the present case can also be **distinguished** from those of a precedent in such a way as to show that the precedent does not apply. Finally, a higher court may **disapprove** of a precedent thereby indicating that it will be overruled when an opportunity arises.

Advantages and Disadvantages of the system of Judicial Precedent

The **advantages** may be summarised as follows:-

1. **Certainty** — If there were no precedents it would be impossible to predict the outcome of a case. It is desirable that people should be able to order their affairs confidently on the basis of settled law.
2. The law develops out of **real cases** involving real problems, it is not based on some academic theory.
3. **Flexibility** — Through the processes of distinguishing and overruling the law can develop to meet changing and social conditions.

The **disadvantages** may be summarised as follows:-

1. In spite of the processes of distinguishing and overruling, the system tends to **rigidity**. It is a long and expensive procedure to challenge a precedent.
2. The development of the law is **slow.** It depends upon the willingness of people to litigate with all the anxiety and expense which that entails.
3. The process of distinguishing leads to much **complexity** and a great bulk of law reports.

1.14 CUSTOM

A custom is a rule which has existed or is presumed to have existed from time immemorial and which has the force of law in a particular locality.

Custom is therefore an unwritten exception to the common law. As a source of law, custom is of minor importance but the courts may recognise a custom if the following conditions are fulfilled:

1. The custom must have existed from **time immemorial** which, conveniently means from 1189! It is for the person who alleges that such a custom exists to bring evidence of it. If he establishes sufficient evidence, he is then helped by the presumption that the custom has been in existence since 1189. The effect of the presumption is to transfer the burden of proof to the person who alleges that no such custom exists, i.e. the opponent must disprove the existence of the custom.

   This process is illustrated by the case of **Mercer -v- Denne** (1905) in which it was asserted by the local fishermen that they had a customary right to dry their nets upon part of a beach owned by Denne. The problem was that Denne wanted to have some houses built on this piece of land and would thus have prevented the drying of the nets. It was proved in evidence that this custom went back 70 years and doubtless longer. Thus the presumption arose in favour of the fishermen and Denne was not allowed to build the houses.

2. The custom must have been **enjoyed continuously** since time immemorial i.e. the right to exercise the custom must have been enjoyed without lawful interruption.
3. The custom must have been exercised **peacefully, openly and as of right.** There must be no question of permission having been given by anybody or of a furtive or forcible exercise as such would be inconsistent with the concept of a "right".
4. The custom must **not be unreasonable** this is a matter for the courts to assess.
5. The custom must be **certain.**
6. The custom must be **compulsory,** i.e. legally binding upon those who use it.
7. The custom must **not be inconsistent** with other customs.
8. The custom must **not be contrary to statue law.**
9. The custom must be **genuinely local,** i.e. apply to a certain area.

SUMMARY

SOURCES OF LAW

- Common Law (i.e. case law through the system of judicial precedent)
- Equity
- Custom
- Statutes
  - includes delegated legislation
- E.E.C. Law

JUDICIAL PRECEDENT: THE HIERARCHY OF THE COURTS

- **Civil Courts**
  - House of Lords
    - Court of Appeal (Civil Division)
      - High Court
        - Queen Bench
        - Family
        - Chancery
          - County Court
- **Judicial Committee of the Privy Council**
- **Criminal Courts**
  - House of Lords
    - Court of Appeal (Criminal Division)
      - Crown Court
        - Magistrates' Court

CHAPTER 2.

THE ENGLISH LEGAL SYSTEM

CATEGORIES OF LAW

2.01 English law divides into two categories: **civil law** and **criminal law.**

In broad terms, the purpose of **civil law** is to **compensate** the victim of a civil wrong; the purpose of the **criminal law** is to **punish** an offender. Thus civil law is concerned with the resolution of disputes between individuals; criminal law is concerned with society punishing a person for breaking its law.

In order to differentiate between these two categories, a different terminology is used for each. A criminal case would be referred to as, e.g. R v Smith. R stand for Rex (King) or Regina (Queen), i.e. the Crown and Smith stands for the defendant. The 'v' stands for 'versus', 'against'. The defendant is also referred to as the 'accused'. One speaks of a person having committed an 'offence', of a 'charge' being brought, then of a 'prosecution'. If the accused is found 'guilty', he is then 'convicted' and 'sentenced'. A civil case would be referred to as, e.g. Jones -v- Smith: the first name is that of the plaintiff, i.e. the person who brings the action and the second name is that of the defendant, i.e. the person against whom the action is brought. The names can be reversed on appeal: the person who brings the appeal is called the 'appellant' and the person against whom the appeal is brought is called the 'respondent'.

2.02 Most **criminal cases** are dealt with by the **Magistrates Court,** but the more **serious offences** are dealt with by the **Crown Court**. The document which marks the commencement of proceedings in the Magistrates Court is called a 'summons'; in the Crown Court, the corresponding document is called an 'indictment'.

2.03 Most **civil cases** are dealt with by the **County Court,** but those where the sum of money or value of property involved exceeds a certain limit are dealt with by the **High Court.** The usual document which marks the commencement of proceedings in the County Court is a **'summons'**; in the High Court, the corresponding document is called a **'writ'.**

2.04 Another important difference between criminal and civil cases is the standard of proof required. In a criminal case, the burden of proof is borne by the Crown, i.e. the prosecution. It is a fundamental principle of our law that an accused person is presumed innocent unless and until proved guilty. Therefore the prosecution must adduce, i.e. bring, evidence to prove that its allegations are true. The standard to which the prosecution must prove its case is a high one: it must prove beyond reasonable doubt that the accused person committed the offence with which he is charged. If the Crown fails to do so, in the opinion of the magistrates or a jury, then the accused must be acquitted. In a civil case, the burden of proof is normally borne by the plaintiff on the principle that the person who makes an allegation must prove it. However, the standard of proof is not so exacting as for a criminal trial; the plaintiff's claim will succeed if he can prove his case on a **balance of probabilities.**

2.05 Some facts give rise only to an offence, e.g. owning a television without a T.V. licence; some facts give rise only to a civil wrong, e.g. a breach of contract. However, there are facts which give rise to both crimes and civil wrongs, e.g. driving a car in such a manner as to cause injury to someone might be the offence of driving without due care and attention and also the civil wrong or tort of negligence. Similarly, a misdescription of goods might be an offence under the **Trade Description Acts** and a civil wrong under the **Sale of Goods Act 1979.**

2.06 Criminal offences range from parking offences, and failure to take out a licence where required, to murder, rape and arson. The Civil Law divides into several branches, **contract** which is concerned with legally binding agreement, **torts** which is concerned with duties imposed by law upon persons in their relations to others; **trusts** which is concerned with the administration of property by trustees for the benefit of a person called a beneficiary; **family law** which is concerned with divorce, division of property between spouses on divorce and custody of children; the **law of property** which is concerned mainly with freeholds and leaseholds. There are other more specialised branches, e.g. **marine law** and **insurance law.**

2.07 **Liability**

In English law liability does not normally arise unless the defendant is in some way at fault, i.e. there must be some form of wrong-doing for which he is responsible.

In the law of TORTS, the defendant will not normally be liable to compensate the plaintiff unless the defendant is in some way blame-worthy, e.g. he has failed to take proper care in a situation in which the law places him under a duty to take care, and, as a result of his failure, the plaintiff suffers some form of harm, e.g. injury to person or damage to property. However, there are exceptions to the rule that liability is based on fault. These exceptions occur in situations where the law holds the defendant **strictly liable** for the damage which occurs. A form of strict liability is **vicarious liability** (i.e. the liability of one person for the torts of another). Thus an employer is said to be vicariously liable for the torts committed by his employee during the course of the employee's employment. This means that if the employee negligently injures someone, the employer can be sued for damages by the injured person. The employer may be in no way blameworthy but he is nevertheless liable.

2.08 In CONTRACT, liability is **strict,** i.e. if the defendant breaks the terms of the agreement, he is liable. It is not necessary for the plaintiff to prove that the defendant was negligent or in any way blameworthy in departing from the terms of the contract.

2.09 Just as there is a strong moral basis to liability in the law of torts, so there is a strong moral basis to liability in the CRIMINAL LAW. In other words a person will not be found guilty of a crime unless he is blameworthy. It is thus a fundamental common law principle of criminal law that **two** elements have to be proved by the prosecution before the accused will be convicted of the crime with which he is charged: the **actus reus** and the **mens rea.** The actus reus means 'wrongful act', i.e. the act which is prohibited by law. For murder, the actus reus is the unlawful killing. The mens rea is the 'guilty mind', i.e. the intention to do the wrongful act or a reckless state of mind, i.e. an attitude of 'not caring less' whether the wrongful act occurs or not. The mens rea of murder is malice aforethought, i.e. an intention to kill or cause grevious bodily harm. The difference between murder and manslaughter lies not in the actus reus which is identical in both cases, but in the mens rea; in manslaughter there is an absence of malice aforethought, e.g. because the accused acted under provocation from his victim or because he was performing an illegal operation, e.g. an abortion not within the terms of the **Aborition Law Reform Act 1967,** and death happened to occur during the course of it.

2.10 Some statutory offences are offences of **strict liability,** i.e. no mens rea has to be proved by the prosecution. Most statutory provisions relating to licences come into this category, e.g. failure to hold a television licence where one is required consistutes the offence irrespective of the state of mind of the person charged. In the **Licensing Act 1964 S.172(3)** states "The holder of a justices' licence shall not sell intoxicating liquor to a drunken person." The wording is absolute, i.e. the licensee will commit an offence if alcohol is sold to a drunken person whether he knows of the sale or not. Thus the licensee was convicted where a barman contrary to instructions served a drunken person in **Commissioners of Police for the Metropolis -v- Cartman** (1896). The judge declared that the purpose of the statutory provision was to maintain public order and therefore no defence was open to the publican.

2.11 In certain circumstances, **persons** may be **excused from criminal liability** as follows:-

1. **The Insane**

   In order that insanity should amount to a defence, the accused must prove on a balance of probabilities that he is insane within the meaning of the **McNaughton Rules,** i.e. that he does not know the nature and quality of his act or, if he does know it, he does not know that it is wrong. If the defence succeeds, the verdict will be 'not guilty by reason of insanity'. It is possible, of course, than an insane person is found 'unfit to plead' before the trial in which case he can be committed to a special hospital. He can also be transferred to a mental hospital during or after the trial.

It should be noted that there is a special defence to murder of 'diminished responsibility' introduced by the **Homicide Act 1957.** In order for the defence to succeed, the accused must prove that he was suffering from such abnormality of mind as to result in substantial impairment of his responsibility for his actions. The effect of a successful defence is to reduce the killing from murder to manslaughter. The convicted person is then committed to prison, at least initially, rather than to a mental hospital.

2. **Those suffering from Drunkenness**
Drunkenness is not in itself a defence to any crime unless it is to such a degree as to amount to insanity within the McNaghten Rules. However, it may have the effect that the accused is in fact incapable of forming the mens rea of the particular offence. If a person drinks in order to give himself 'dutch courage' before committing an offence, he will, of course, be fully liable.

3. **Minors**
There is an irrebutable presumption of law (i.e. it is not possible to bring evidence to prove the contrary) that children aged under ten years are incapable of committing a crime. There is a rebutable presumption that children aged between ten and fourteen years are incapable of forming the mens rea required for an offence. Thus, in this instance, the prosecution may bring evidence to show that the particular accused child was sufficiently mentally mature as to possess the necessary mens rea. Young persons over the age of fourteen years have full criminal responsibility, but their punishments are different from those of adults.

4. Those acting **under Duress or Compulsion**
Where the person charges with an offence acted under physical force exerted upon him by someone else, he will be excused from liability. It is probable that the mere threat of violence does not amount to lawful excuse. It is certainly no defence to murder or treason that the accused acted through fear induced by threats.

5. Those acting under a **Mistake**
A mistake of law is never a defence. A mistake of fact can amount to a defence if it is reasonable, e.g. the picking up of someone else's umbrella in the belief that it is one's own as the umbrellas are virtually identical and were left in the same place.

6. Those acting from **Necessity**
Necessity is not a defence known in English law. This was established in the famous case of **R -v- Dudley and Stevens** (1844) in which some ship-wrecked mariners killed and ate the cabin boy in a desperate attempt to keep themselves from starving.

2.12 **Remedies and Punishments**
In **civil actions,** one speaks of the innocent party obtaining redress or having a remedy granted by the court for the wrong which he has suffered. For breach of contract there is a remedy of **damages** or the equitable remedies of **recission, specific performance,** or **rectification.** Similarly the victim of a tort is awarded damages and/or an injunction.

In **criminal cases,** a punishment is imposed upon the convicted person. It is sometimes not realised that the death sentence is still retained for treason. Imprisonment is, of course, the form of sentence for other serious crimes. An important development in our law was the introduction of the suspended sentence by the **Criminal Justice Act 1967.** If the convicted person does not commit any further crime punishable by imprisonment during the period of suspension, the suspended sentence will never be served. Fines are self-explanatory, but they do not help the victim as the fine goes to the Crown. For this reason, **The Powers of Criminal Courts Act 1973** enpowers criminal courts to make limited compensation orders in favour of the victim. There are special forms of punishment for young persons such as youth custody for offences which would have been punishable by imprisonment if committed by adults, detention in a Detention Centre, supervision orders and the "short sharp shock" treatment in certain Detention Centres. Probation, cannot, of course, be classified as a punishment: its object being to set the convicted person on the road to improvement. Similarly, Community Service Orders introduced by the **Powers of Criminal Courts Act 1973** have a constructive aim.

2.13 Finally, it may be noted that the court can record a conviction without imposing any form of punishment with an **absolute** or a **conditional discharge.** The condition attached to the latter is that no further offence be committed within a certain period. An absolute discharge is, of course, free of any condition.

THE COURTS

2.14 THE CRIMINAL COURTS are as follows:-

a) **The Magistrates' Court**
As previously mentioned, most criminal cases are dealt with by this court. It is usually composed of a bench of three magistrates, one of whom acts as chairman. They are laypersons appointed by the Lord Chancellor and are chosen for their personal qualities, not for their legal knowledge. They

are assisted by a **Clerk to the court** who is legally qualified and whose task is to advise them on the relevant law. In large towns, there is a **stipendiary** magistrate, i.e. a full-time paid lawyer. The Magistrates Court has two main functions: **it tries the less serious criminal offences** and it holds **preliminary hearings** of the more serious offences in order to see whether there is sufficient evidence for the case to go to trial before judge and jury at the Crown Court. There is an intermediate category of offences which are triable either summarily, i.e. before the magistrates or on **indictment.** i.e. before the Crown Court. The accused has the right to elect, i.e. choose the form of trial. However, if the magistrates convict the accused following summary trial and find, after hearing details of any previous convictions, that they have insufficient power to punish him appropriately, they may refer him to the Crown Court for sentencing. It should, of course, be remembered that a high percentage of pleas before the Magistrates' Court are guilty pleas. In these cases, the role of the defence is merely to make a speech in mitigation, i.e. to outline to the Crown personal factors, such as domestic problems and illness, which the Court should take into account in deciding upon the sentence.

An **appeal** against conviction or sentence lies to the **Crown Court** where there is a complete re-trial. If the appeal is on a point of law, it is made by way of **'case-stated'** to the Queen's Bench Division of the High Court. This means that the magistrates state facts and the Q.B.D. then decides the point of law involved. The case is then remitted, i.e. sent back, to the magistrates for a decision by applying the law as stated to the facts.

b) **The Juvenile Court**

The Juvenile Court is composed of magistrates and its function is to deal with offences, except for the most serious, committed by young persons, i.e. those aged between 14 and 17 years and by children, i.e. those aged 10 to 14 years. The public are excluded from the hearing so as to protect the accused from publicity. The proceedings are more informal than before the ordinary Magistrates Court.

c) **The Crown Court**

The Crown Court deals with the more serious offences and those where the accused elects for trial on indictment. **Circuit Judges** and **Recorders** try the lesser offences: **High Court Judges** try the more serious and most serious offences. There is a jury of twelve laypersons.

An appeal against conviction of sentence lies to the **Court of Appeal (Criminal Division).**

d) **The Court of Appeal (Criminal Division)**

The court is composed of three judges called **Lords Justice of Appeal.** The senior judge being the **Lord Chief Justice.** The court's sole function is to decide appeals, but it can order a re-trial.

A final appeal where a point of law of general public importance is involved lies to **The House of Lords.**

e) **The House of Lords**
A full court is composed of five Law Lords or, to give them their full title, **Lords of Appeal in Ordinary.** A quorum is three Law Lords, Leave, i.e. permission, of either the Court of Appeal of the Appellate Committee of The House of Lords is required before an appeal can be brought.

f) **The Coroners' Courts**
These are special courts quite separate from the ones described above. They are presided over by a coroner who is a barrister, solicitor or medical practitioner. In some cases, a jury is required. The function of these courts is to enquire into the cause of unnatural deaths and to deal with treasure trove.

2.15 **THE CIVIL COURTS** are as follows:-

a) **The County Court**
This court deals with the majority of civil cases. It is presided over by a circuit judge and has jurisdiction, i.e. power to deal with cases where the sum of money involved or the value of the property involved does not exceed a certain sum, e.g. a claim **not exceeding £5,000** in **contract** or **tort.** The court can try cases where the appropriate limit is exceeded with the agreement of both parties, Jurisdiction varies between County Courts, e.g. some have power to deal with undefended divorces, others have not. **Small Claims,** i.e. those involving not more than £500, are usually referred to the County Court **arbitration scheme.** The **Registrar** normally acts as arbitrator. The Registrar is responsible for administrative matters of the Courts and has a more limited jurisdiction than the judge. However, he can deal with matters where the sum involved exceeds £500 with the agreement of both parties. Use of the arbitration procedure is encouraged by the fact that a successful plaintiff cannot claim the costs of legal representation against the defendant where the sum involved does not exceed £500. It is therefore in his interests to save money by representing himself at the arbitration where formalities are kept to a minimum. However, the plaintiff can claim limited 'fixed costs' which vary according to the sum involved. An appeal against a decision of the County Court lies to the **Court of Appeal (Civil Division)** save that some appeals are heard by the special Divisional Courts of the High Court, e.g. an appeal in bankruptcy proceedings would go to the Divisional Court of the Chancery Division.

b) **The High Court**
The High Court consists of three main courts of first instance, i.e. courts in which a case is first heard. These are The **Family Division,** The **Chancery Division** and The **Queen's Bench Division.**

The **Family Division** deals with defended divorces, custody of children, division of property between ex-spouses following divorce, non-contentious probate, i.e. where there is no dispute about the will of the deceased, and related matters.

The **Chancery Division** is the modern successor to the old court of Chancery. It deals with matters which fall within the province of Equity, e.g. trusts, contentious probate (i.e. where there is a dispute about the will of the deceased), company law and partnership and real property. A case in the division is designated by the prefix 'Re', e.g. **Re: McArdle.**

The Queen's Bench Division deals with all cases which do not fall within the jurisdiction of either The Family Division or The Chancery Division, notably breaches of contract and torts involving sums of money or value in excess of the County Court limits. There are also some special Courts within the structure, e.g. The **Commercial Court** which deals with technical, commercial disputes and insurance matters, The **Admirality Court** and the **Bankruptcy Court.**

The **Divisional Courts** of The High Court are different from the main divisions mentioned above. A Divisional Court is composed of two or three High Court Judges whereas the main Division has one trial judge. Its function is to hear appeals on points of law by way of case-stated from inferior courts, e.g. from the Licensing Justices. The main Divisions, as mentioned, are Courts where a trial takes place, i.e. where a case originates.

Before we leave the topic of The High Court, it is important to note the special jurisdiction of The Divisional of Queen's Bench. This court, of prestigious status, has supervisory jurisdiction over inferior courts and tribunals. It exercises this jurisdiction by means of the following ancient orders or decrees:-

Mandamus — this means literally 'we command' and is used to compel a public body to carry out a duty, e.g. to order a local authority to produce its accounts for inspection by a rate-payer.

Prohibition — this order prevents an inferior court or tribunal from exceeding its jurisdiction.

Certiorai — this means literally to 'certify' and it is used to quash, i.e. nullify, the decision of an inferior court or tribunal which has been made in excesss of jurisdiction or where the rules of natural justice have been infringed, e.g. where one party was not given a fair hearing because he was not given proper notice of the proceedings and was therefore unable to attend; or where there was bias in the proceedings because those who sat in judgment had an interest in the outcome.

Habeas Corpus — this is the ancient order which ensures that a person is not unlawfully deprived on his liberty. This application takes precedence over all other business. In recent years rather than make application for a specific order, there is a general application for "judicial review".

Appeals from the Divisional Courts go directly to the House of Lords; most appeals from the main Divisions go to the Court of Appeal (Civil Division).

c) **The Court of Appeal (Civil Division)**
This court is composed of three Lords Justice of Appeal. It hears appeals from the County Court and the High Court. Decisions can be made by the majority, i.e. with one judge dissenting. An appeal from this court lies to the House of Lords.

d) **The House of Lords**
This is the final court of appeal in the United Kingdom. A full court is composed of five Lords of Appeal in Ordinary ('Law Lords'). Three Law Lords constitutes a quorum. Decisions can be made by a majority. Leave of either the Court of Appeal or of the Judicial Committee of The House of Lords is required before an appeal can be brought. It should be noted that an appeal can be brought directly to the House of Lords from the decision of the High Court by use of the 'Leapfrog' procedure introduced by the **Administration of Justice Act 1969.** The main condition to be fulfilled before the procedure can be used is that the trial judge grants a certificate stating that the case involves a point of law of general public importance. The procedure is appropriate where one of the parties wishes to challenge a precedent which is binding on the Court of Appeal.

Since the entry of the UK into the EEC, the House of Lords **must** refer any point of Community Law which has not previously been decided to the European Court of Justice under Article 177 of the Treaty of Rome. Courts below the House of Lords **may** make such a reference, but they do not have to do so.

e) **The European Court of Justice**
The Court is composed of judges drawn from each of the EEC countries. It is the final authority on points of Community Law, it decides disputes between member states, and adjudicates in cases of infringement of the Treaties and secondary legislation. Its decisions have to be enforced by the national courts as it has no enforcement procedure of its own.

f) **The Judicial Committee of the Privy Council**
This body is not strictly part of our Court system; it is a body which advises the Sovereign and therefore delivers an opinion rather than a decision. However, it is composed of the Law Lords who staff the House of Lords. Therefore, the Committee's decisions are accorded the utmost respect and it creates very strongly persuasive precedents. It hears appeals from those few remaining Commonwealth countries which have not abolished the right of appeal and also from Prize Courts, Ecclesiastical Courts, Courts of the Isle of Man, the Channel Islands, British Colonies and Protectorates and Tribunals of the medical and dental professions.

g) **Administrative Tribunals**

These are bodies which work parallel to the Civil Courts and adjudicate on disputes within certain special areas as indicated by their titles, e.g. Rent Tribunals, the Lands Tribunal, Industrial Tribunals. They are usually composed of people with specialised knowledge, e.g. an Industrial Tribunal is composed of a person who is drawn from the employer's side of industry, a person who is drawn from the employees' side, e.g. a trade union official and a legally qualified chairman. Their procedure is similar to that of a court, but they are somewhat less formal and the parties often appear in person rather than be represented by lawyers. They are encouraged to do so by the fact that legal aid is not available, save before some tribunals which hear appeals, e.g. the Employment Appeal Tribunal which has High Court status.

The **advantages** of tribunals are said to be their speed, relative cheapness, informality and expert knowledge.

The **disadvantages** of tribunals are said to be the fact that some tribunals are held in private and therefore justice is not "seen to be done"; the danger of lack of impartiality as where a civil servant adjudicates in a dispute to which his department is a party; the fact that there is generally no legal aid so that inarticulate people may be at a disadvantage when representing themselves. In addition some tribunals have a very wide discretion.

In view of the dangers inherent in the system of tribunals there are certain safeguards. There is a statutory body called the Council on Tribunals which examines the working of certain tribunals and reports to The Lord Chancellor. Judicial control is exercised through the ultra vires rule. Ultra vires means, literally, 'beyond the powers'; if a tribunal has acted ultra vires, it means that it has exceeded its powers or infringed the rules of natural justice and accordingly its decision is quashed, i.e. cancelled, by the court, namely The Divisional Court of the Queen's Bench Division of the High Court.

h) **Domestic Tribunals** are bodies such as Trade Unions, the governing bodies of the medical, dental and opticians professions. If a member of one of these bodies infringes its rule, he can have some penalty invoked against him. Therefore the tribunal will be acting quasi-judicially (i.e. in the same way as a judge) in reaching a decision on the evidence. The decision can be challenged in the ordinary courts and declared ultra vires if the powers of the tribunal have been exceeded or abused.

i) **Arbitration**

This is a method of resolving disputes without the parties going to court. It is cheaper and quicker than a court hearing but, perhaps its chief advantage is that it is conducted in private and therefore saves the parties potentially damaging publicity. The arbitrator is also normally an expert in the subject matter of the dispute. For these reasons most written contracts contain an arbitration clause. However, arbitration is a legal proceeding and is therefore subject to the provisions of the Arbitration Acts 1950-1979.

Note that the system of "Small Claims Arbitration" operates within the County Court with regard to claims involving less than £500 (there are current proposals to increase this limit to £1,000).

Civil Law

Contract, Tort, Property, Family
Trusts, Succession etc.

Disputes between Individuals
e.g. Jones -v- Smith

On a balance of probabilities

Damages or Equitable Remedy

County Court

Cases below certain financial limits

High Court

QBD — Family — Chancery

— cases above certain financial limits

Divisional Courts of High Court

— appeals only

Court of Appeal (Civil Division)
— appeals from County Court and High Court

House of Lords

— appeals only

Criminal Law

Examples: Murder, Rape, Arson, Theft,
Fraud, Motoring offences

Technical Offences, e.g. Trade
Descriptions Acts.

Offences punishable by State
e.g. R -v- Smith

Beyond all reasonable doubt

Punishment

Magistrates' Court

— summary offences.
— indictable offences where accused has exercised right
— of election for summary trial.
— preliminary hearings of other indictable offences.

Crown Court

— indictable offences
— appeals from Magistrates' Courts

Court of Appeal (Criminal Division)
— appeals from Crown Court

House of Lords

— appeals only

Various Administrative Tribunals

European Court of Justice

— cases involving points of Community Law
not previously decided.

Judicial Committee of Privy Council

— appeals from
Colonies and Commonwealth Countries
that have retained the right of appeal

— also appeals from
Prize Courts
Ecclesiastical Courts
Medical, dental and opticians tribunals.

Appeals

	Most Civil Appeals	**Some Civil Appeals**	**Criminal Appeals**
	House of Lords	House of Lords	House of Lords
Leapfrog procedure		Court of Appeal	Court of Appeal (Criminal Division)
	Court of Appeal (Civil Divison)	High Court QBD Family Chancery	Crown Court
	County Court	County Court	Magistrates' Court

Civil Liability:
Based on fault in tort with some cases of strict liability in contract

Criminal Liability:
Based on fault with some cases of strict liability

CHAPTER 3.

THE JUDICIARY AND LEGAL PROFESSION

THE LEGAL PROFESSION

3.01 The term 'lawyer' embraces both **Solicitors** and **Barristers**. There are a number of differences between these two branches of the profession and these may be summarised as follows:-

1. Solicitors are with some exceptions, general practioners who deal directly with the client. Barristers are, after a period of practical experience, specialists and are primarily advocates. They receive instructions only through solicitors who 'brief' them.
2. Solicitors have only limited rights of audience before the courts i.e. they may plead before the Magistrates Court, the County Court and in some circumstances, before the Crown Court. Barristers have unlimited rights of audience.
3. A Solicitor is an officer of the Court, his full title being 'Solicitor of the Supreme Court' — a Barrister is not an officer of the court.
4. Solicitors may enter into partnership, i.e. run their business as a firm (but not a limited company); Barristers may not operate in this manner but they often share chambers and a clerk.
5. Solicitors who wish to practise must hold a Practising Certificate issued annually by their governing body the Law Society. A Barrister must be a member of one of the four Inns of Court.
6. Solicitors are bound by rules of the Law Society made under its powers conferred by the Solicitors Act 1974; Barristers are bound by the rules of their Inn of Court.
7. Solicitors who are guilty of 'misconduct' or who infringe the Law Society's accounting rules can be disciplined by the Solicitor's Disciplinary Tribunal, a statutory body with power to fine a Solicitor, suspend him from practice or recommend that he be struck of the Roll. (The Roll is the Roll held by the Master of the Rolls on to which the Solicitor's name was entered when he was admitted as a Solicitor). A Barrister can be disciplined by the Senate of the Inns of Court in similar circumstances.
8. A curious difference is that Solicitors can make a binding contract with their clients, whereas Barristers cannot enter into a binding contract with a Solicitor. However, a Barrister who finds that a Solicitor fails to pay his fees can make a complaint to the Law Society.

In addition to the above there are detailed differences in training between the two branches of the profession.

Both branches of the profession enjoy immunity from being sued in respect of statements made in court, i.e. they could not be sued for slander as their statements are absolutely privileged.

Note that the Government has recently issued several consultative (or "Green Papers") containing radical proposals for reform of both branches of the legal profession involving changes which many lawyers are opposing. The proposals, it is argued, would introduce elements of greater competition but opponents argue that such changes are not in the "public interest".

3.02 **Judges**

The Judges are drawn from the ranks of practising Barristers in particular from eminent Barristers who have been appointed **Queen's Counsel** by the Lord Chancellor, a process known as 'taking silk' after the silk gown worn by a Q.C. There is a hierarchy within the judiciary, just as there is a hierarchy within the courts:-

3.03 **Recorders**

Recorders are the most junior members of the judiciary. They are appointed by the Lord Chancellor from Barristers and Solicitors of at least ten years standing. They act as part-time Judges in the County Court and they try the less serious offences in the Crown Court with a jury.

3.04 **Circuit Judges-**

Circuit Judges are appointed by the Lord Chancellor from Barristers of at least seven years standing or from Recorders who have served for at least three years. Thus Solicitors may become Circuit Judges after having served as Recorders. These Judges try issues in the County Court and all but the most serious cases in the Crown Court. In the latter instance, they sit with a jury. Like Recorders, Circuit Judges can be dismissed from office by the Lord Chancellor for misconduct or incapacity.

3.05 **High Court Judges**

High Court Judges are appointed by the Crown on the recommendation of the Lord Chancellor from Barristers of at least ten years standing. They try cases throughout the Divisions of the High Court, including the Divisional Courts and also the more serious cases in the Crown Court.

Their status differs fundamentally from that of Recorders and Circuit Judges in that they cannot be removed from office under any circumstances by the Lord Chancellor. The only way that they can be removed is by an address to the Crown (i.e. a petition) made by both Houses of Parliament. This constitutes the main safeguard of their independence, i.e. **no** government can remove a Judge because they do not like his judgments.

3.06 **Lords Justice of Appeal**

Lords Justices of Appeal are appointed by the Crown on the recommendation of the Prime Minister from Barristers of at least fifteen years standing or High Court Judges who have served for at least one year. They staff both divisions of the Court of Appeal. In the Civil Division they are presided over by the **Master of the Rolls** and in the Criminal Division by the **Lord Chief Justice.** They can only be removed from office by an address to the Crown by both Houses of Parliament.

3.07 **Lords of Appeal in Ordinary**

This is the full title of the most senior of our Judges, i.e. those who staff the House of Lords. They are most commonly known as Law Lords. They are appointed by the Crown on the recommendation of the Prime Minister from Barristers of at least fifteen years standing or Judges of the High Court or above who have served for at least two years.

3.08 **Judges of the European Court**

There is a Judge for each member state of the E.E.C. sitting under a President. The interesting difference from our own system is that Professors of Law may be appointed as well as members of the judiciary of the member state.

3.09 **Other Holders of Judicial Offices and Appointments**

1. **The Lord Chancellor**
   The Lord Chancellor is head of the judiciary and the senior Judge of the House of Lords: he is also a member of the Government and indeed, a member of the Cabinet. However, he is strictly impartial in his judicial capacity, i.e. he never allows political considerations to influence him in spite of his dual role.
2. **The Vice-Chancellor**
   In theory, the Lord Chancellor is head of the Chancery Division of the High Court, but, in practice, it is presided over by the Vice-Chancellor.
3. **The Lord Chief Justice**
   The Lord Chief Justice presides over the Court of Appeal (Criminal Division) and over the Queen's Bench Division of the High Court.
4. **The President of the Family Division of the High Court**
   This title is self explanatory.
5. **The Master of the Rolls**
   The Master of the Rolls is head of the Court of Appeal (Civil Division). He is also in charge of the Court Rolls or records, hence his title. When a person qualifies as a Solicitor, his name is admitted to the Roll by the Master of the Rolls.
6. **Master of the Supreme Court**
   Masters of the Supreme Court deal with the 'behind the scenes' work of

the High Court. In particular they deal with interlocutory matters, i.e. matters arising in the course of preparation of a case for trial and with the taxation of costs. 'Taxation' means assessment of costs payable.

7. **Law Officers of the Crown**

(a) **The Attorney-General**

The Attorney-General is a Barrister and member of the Government. He advises the Government on matters of law and has various other functions. In particular, he brings the most important prosecutions on behalf of the Crown. His 'fiat', i.e. permission, is required before certain types of prosecution can be brought, e.g. for incest and under the **Official Secrets Act 1911.** He is also the only person who can stop a criminal trial by entering a nolle prosequi. He is leader of the Bar and overseas the work of the Director of Public Prosecutions.

(b) **The Solicitor-General**

The Solicitor-General is in fact a Barrister and his function is to assist the Attorney-General and deputise when necessary.

8. **The Director of Public Prosecutions**

The D.P.P. is a Barrister or Solicitor and is a Civil Servant. His duty is to bring important or difficult prosecutions on behalf of the Crown and to advise police forces in individual cases.

9. **Coroners**

A Coroner is a Solicitor or Barriser or Medical Practioner of at least five years standing. His duties are to enquire into the causes of unnatural deaths and to deal with treasure trove.

10. **Registrars**

Registrars are assistant Judges in the County Courts and, unlike all other judges, they are Civil Servants. Their main jurisdiction is in cases in which the amount involved does not exceed £500. However, they can deal with cases where the sum exceeds £500 with the consent of both parties. Registrars usually act as arbitrators under the County Court arbitration scheme.

3.10 **Laypersons**

Laypersons have played an important part in our legal system from an early time.

Magistrates or Justices of the Peace

Magistrates or J.P.'s are usually laypersons, but in the larger towns there are full-time **stipendiary** or paid magistrates.

Lay Magistrates are appointed by the Lord Chancellor from among persons of good character who are recommended by the Lord Lientenant of a County or the Council of a Borough. A bench of Magistrates consists of at least two persons and more commonly three persons one of whom acts as chairman. They are adivsed on the law by a clerk. A stipendiary Magistrate is appointed by the Crown on the recommendation of the Lord Chancellor and sits alone.

Magistrates may be removed from office by the Lord Chancellor for incompetence or misconduct.

3.11 **Jurors**

Jurors are chosen at random from the Electoral Register from persons aged between 18 and 65 years. The following categories of persons are not, however, eligible to serve:-

Clergymen, Mental Patients, Judges, Solicitors, Barristers, Policemen and others concerned with the administration of justice.

Certain categories of convicted criminals.

The following categories of persons are eligible to serve, but can claim exemption as of right:-

Members of the House of Commons or House of Lords, Members of the Armed Services, Medical practitioners, Persons who have served on a jury within the last two years.

Persons eligible for jury service receive a summons to attend and are subject to penalties if they fail to do so. However, those who would face special hardship can request to be excused service, e.g. mothers of young children.

Jurors serve in both civil and criminal trials and their duty is to judge the case on the evidence. The judge interprets the law and the jury judges the facts. Thus it is for the jury to decide whether or not the evidence of a witness is credible. A jury is rarely found in a civil case with the exception of actions involving fraud or defamation in the High Court, (e.g. libel cases).

These cases involve serious allegations affecting the character of a person and a jury is a suitable tribunal. Trials in the Crown Court always take place in the presence of a jury. Thus the most important role of the jury is to acquit or return a verdict of 'guilty' in a criminal trial.

Before a trial begins, a jury is empanelled, i.e. sworn in. Initially the number is twelve, but it may fall to eleven, ten or nine through illness or accidents. If the number falls below nine, a retrial may be ordered. A jury should strive to reach a unanimous decision, but it may return a majority decision after due deliberation of ten out of a jury of eleven or twelve or nine out of jury of ten. In a criminal trial an accused person has a right of challenge if he can give good reason, e.g. that he knows the juror personally. The right of peremptory challenge has now been abolished.

3.12 **Legal Aid and Legal Advice and Assistance**

The law relating to legal aid and legal advice and assistance is contained in the **Legal Aid Acts 1974 and 1979** and in regulations made under these acts. The purpose of the Legal Advice and Assistance Scheme (known as the green form scheme) is to enable people to obtain the help of a Solicitor with a legal problem, but it does not cover the institution or conduct of court proceedings. It does, however, cover representation in most domestic proceedings in Magistrates Courts. It is means-tested and the means of the applicant are assessed by the Solicitor on a green form.

Legal Aid is available for both civil and criminal proceedings. The Legal Aid Scheme is administered by the Legal Aid Board: applications are made to local committees with a right of appeal against a refusal to an area committee. Applications are scrutinized to see whether the applicant qualifies on financial grounds and whether he has a sound case. If the committee is satisfied that the applicant qualifies, a legal aid certificate is eventually issued.

If the applicant's disposable capital and disposable income are below a certain limit no contribution towards legal costs is required from him; if his disposable capital and disposable income exceed a certain limit he will not be eligible for legal aid, between the lower and upper limits he will be required to make a contribution. Statements as to means made by the applicant are verified by the Department of Health and Social Security.

In criminal cases, there are no strict financial limits and the accused's means are normally assessed after the hearing. If the accused did not make an application for legal aid prior to the commencement of the proceedings, he may apply to the court which has power to make a legal aid order.

It should be understood that legal aid is not free in the sense that treatment under the National Health Service is free to the person receiving it. If an assisted litigant is unsuccessful in a civil action, the legal aid fund must be reimbursed the costs which it has had to bear. This may come from award of costs against the party who loses the case. However, if the costs recovered, together with the successful party's contribution are insufficient to reimburse the fund in full, the Legal Aid Board has a first charge on any property preserved or recovered in the action. This means that the successful litigant's award of damages may be reduced by the balance of costs to be reimbursed. If the property preserved or recovered is a house, e.g. in matrimonial proceedings, it may well be encumbered with the statutory charge in favour of the Legal Aid Board, i.e. when it is sold the sum secured must be repaid to the Legal Aid Board.

SUMMARY AND DIAGRAMS

The Judges

House of Lords

Lords of Appeal in Ordinary
(The Law Lords)

Senior Judge: Lord Chancellor

Court of Appeal (Civil Division)

Lord Justices of Appeal

Senior Judge: Master of the Rolls

Court of Appeal (Criminal Division)

Lord Justices of Appeal

Senior Judge: Lord Chief Justice

High Court

High Court or Puisne Justice
in

Queen's Bench Division	Family Division	Chancery Division
Lord Chief Justice	President	Vice-Chancellor

Crown Court

High Court Judges

Circuit Judges

Recorders

— depending on gravity of case.

County Court

Circuit Judges

Recorders

Registrars

Magistrates' Court

Lay Magistrate

Stipendiary Magistrate

Laypersons who participate in the administration of justice:

Lay Magistrate

Jurors

CHAPTER 4.

LEGAL STATUS AND PERSONALITY

4.01 NATURAL PERSONS

Natural persons under English Law can do anything which is not forbidden by law: that is implicit in our concept of freedom.

Certain persons, however, have a special status and their capacity is limited in various ways by this status. For example, **marriage** brings about a change of status: the husband automatically becomes liable to maintain his wife; a married person cannot marry anyone else whilst still married; a will made before the date of the marriage is normally revoked, i.e. cancelled by the marriage.

Certain persons are said to be under a legal **disability**, e.g. **minors** and the **mentally ill**. Thus a minor, i.e. a person aged under eighteen cannot vote or sit on a jury, or marry without consent. He has only limited capacity to make a contract. He is fully liable in theory for his torts but in reality it is unlikely that an action would be brought against him as he would not have the means to satisfy a judgment. In criminal law, no minor under the age of ten years is capable of a crime: therefore he cannot be prosecuted. Minors aged between ten and fourteen years are incapable of committing a crime unless there is evidence to show that they are mentally capable of the crime in question. Minors over the age of fourteen years are capable of committing crimes in the same way as adults, but their punishments are different. Minors can sue by their **'next friend'** and defend an action by their **'guardian at litem'** i.e. through parent or guardian.

Persons who are mentally ill within the meaning of the **Mental Health Act 1983** are treated similarly to minors in the law of contract and the law of torts. They can sue by their 'next friend' and defend by the 'guardian ad litem'. In criminal law they may lack the mens rea or mental state required for the particular crime. If such a person is found to be insane within the narrow definition of the **MacNaghten rules** i.e. he is found not to know the nature and quality of his act or not to know that it is wrong, he will be found 'not guilty by reason of insanity'.

4.02 CORPORATIONS

A corporation or artificial person is a legal entity of person which is distinct from its members.

There are three main types of corporation: **Chartered Corporations; Statutory Corporations** and **Companies registered under the Companies Acts**.

Chartered Corporations

These are incorporated by Royal Charter, e.g. the Chartered Insurance Institute and many professional bodies, certain Local Authorities, e.g. the City of Gloucester, and other bodies e.g. Universities. If such a corporation exceeds the powers conferred upon it by its charter its acts will be valid, but the charter might be forfeited by the Crown.

Statutory Corporations

These are incorporated by Act of Parliament or statute and they derive their powers strictly from their statute. All the nationalised industries are statutory corporations, e.g. the Gas Corporation, the National Coal Board, the Electricity Council. If this type of corporation exceeds its powers it is said to act **ultra vires** and its act is void. In practice, however, the powers of these corporations are very wide. Recently the Polytechnics and some of the largest public-sector Colleges have been given 'corporate status'.

Companies Registered under the Companies Acts

These can be divided into Unlimited Companies, Companies limited by guarantee and Companies limited by shares.

Unlimited Companies

These are not very common because the members do not enjoy the advantage of limited liability. They are set up, e.g. to run artistic, rather than commercial concerns.

Companies limited by Guarantee

The members act as guarantors, i.e. they each guarantee that in the event of winding-up, the members will contribute a certain sum which may be substantial or merely nominal. Their guarantee is the limit of their liability.

Companies limited by Shares

These can be either **Public Limited Companies** or **Private Companies**.

Public Limited Companies — P.L.C.

A Public Limited Company is a type of company created by the **Companies Act 1980**. It must meet certain capital requirements and if it fails to do so, it automatically becomes a private company. Only a Public Limited Company can issue a prospectus, i.e. invite the public to subscribe for its shares. There must be at least two members and two directors.

Private Companies

A Private Company must have at least two members and one director, but there is no longer a maximum number of members. Such companies no longer have to restrict the transferability of their shares, but may do so if they wish. In practice, most companies will allow transfer of a member's shares only with the consent of the directors so that the founder members can keep control. A private company cannot of course, invite the public to subscribe for its shares. A most important characteristic of both types of company limited by a share capital is that **the members enjoy the privilege of limited liability**.

This means that a shareholder's liability is limited to the nominal value of his shares. The nominal value is the amount printed on the share certificate. It is also called the face or par value. Once this sum is fully paid up, the shareholder has no further responsibility. Thus whilst only part of the sum remains unpaid, the registrar of the company can make a 'call' on the shares i.e. require payment on the balance due.

4.03 **Formation of a Company**

In order to obtain registration of a company, the promoters must deliver to the Registrar of Companies certain items of which the most important are the constitutional documents of the proposed company, namely the Memorandum of Association and the Articles of Association.

The Memorandum of Association

This document regulates the dealings between the company and outsiders, i.e. persons who are not members of the company such as its customers and suppliers.

The most important clause is the objects clause. This sets out the purposes for which the company was set up, e.g. to build properties. It must act within the powers conferred by this clause. If it exceeds those powers, its acts are ultra vires and therefore void. Thus a contract made by a company in excess of its powers would be unenforceable by the company, i.e. the company could not sue on it. However, S.9 (1) **European Communities Act 1972** provides that where an ultra vires contract is decided upon by the directors of the company and is entered into by an outsider in good faith, i.e. without his knowing that the contract is ultra vires, the contract can be enforced, i.e. sued upon, by the outsider even though the company could not sue upon it. Moreover, there is a presumption that an outsider acted in good faith. This means that the company would have to provide evidence of bad faith in order to defeat the presumption.

The Articles of Association

The Articles of the company regulate the **internal dealings** of the company, i.e. they form a contract between each member and all the other members and between the members and the company. They commonly set out the voting rights of shareholders, the powers of the directors and make provision for the election of directors etc.

Companies can be wound up and then struck off the register. In view of the fact that the company continues regardless of the deaths of members, until winding up, it is said to have **'perpetual succession'**.

The types of corporation described above are all 'Corporation Aggregate' because they are the coming together of two or more people in a corporation. There are also 'Corporation Sole', i.e. offices held by an individual, e.g. the Queen, a Bishop of the Church of England, a Vicar. The office holder will die, but the office will continue as a corporation. It is therefore a convenient device for holding property.

4.04 UNINCORPORATED ASSOCIATIONS

These are a collection of people who form an association without incorporating it, e.g. a club or artistic society. Thus the association is not an entity distinct from its members. In practice, there is invariably a committee appointed to run the club or society. The members of the committee are liable for any act which they authorise, e.g. a contract entered into by one of their members after they have a resolution that he should do so. He is also personally liable. The main body of members, i.e. those who are not members of the committee, will only be liable if they have authorised the contract, i.e. by a resolution in general meeting, or if they have ratified it, i.e. adopted it by resolution after it has been made, or if the rules of the association make them liable.

If the committee authorise an act they can also be liable in tort to any one injured, e.g. by the negligent performance of that act. The individual who committed the tort will, of course, be personally liable and in some circumstances the ordinary body of members may be held liable.

4.05 PARTNERSHIPS

These are special forms of unincorporated association which are governed by the **Partnership Act 1890**. S.1 of the Act defines partnership as **"the relationship which subsists between persons carrying on a business in common with a view of profit"**. Thus the difference between, say, a club and a partnership is that the club is carried on without those running it seeking to make a profit whereas a partnership is a way of running a business in order to make a profit. A partnership or firm must have at least two and with some exceptions not more than twenty members.

There are two distinct parts to the Act, one governing the relationship between the partners themselves and the other governing the relationship between the partnership and the outsiders.

The Relationship between the Partners

The provisions of the Act governing the internal dealings of the partners apply only so long as the partners do not agree something contrary to those provisions. Thus the Act provides that each partner has the following rights: to share in the management of the business; to receive an equal share of the profits; to veto the introduction of a new partner; to demand the utmost good faith from his fellow partners.

In practice, it is common for the partners to agree to an unequal sharing of profits etc. They may express their intention in the form of a deed, i.e. Articles of Partnership, or more informally, e.g. in the accounts.

The Relationship between the Partners and Outsiders

The provisions of the Act governing external dealing cannot be altered by agreement between the partners. The reason for this is that they exist for the protection of outsiders, i.e. the firm's creditors and others.

The main facts about a partnership which affect outsiders are:

1. That each partner is liable without limit for all the debts of the firm (therefore any agreement between the partners as to the proportions in which they should share losses does not affect an outsider).
2. Each partner is an agent of the other partners and of the firm in making contracts within the normal scope of the firm's business, i.e. he renders the other partners liable on a normal contract.
3. Each partner is liable for the torts by any other partner committed during the course of the firm's business, i.e. the partners can be ordered by a court to compensate the victim.

4.06 LLOYD'S UNDERWRITERS

Lloyd's Underwriters form a syndicate, i.e. a form of unincorporated association for convenience but they cannot form a partnership. Thus, although an underwriter or 'name' is liable without limit for the proportion of the risk underwritten by him, he is not liable for the proportions underwritten by other underwriters or 'names'. Therefore if his own proportion of the risk is 50% and two other persons are liable for 25% each and fail to honour their commitment he remains liable only for his own 50%.

4.07 TRADE UNIONS

Although Trade Unions are classified as unincorporated associations, they have many of the characteristics of corporations. They can sue and be sued in their own name. The immunity in tort which they enjoyed under the **Trade Union and Labour Relations Acts 1974** and **1976** is not much restricted by the **Employment Acts** of **1980, 1982** and **1986-88**. Where the Union 'authorises or endorses' unlawful action by its members, it renders itself liable in tort for their actions, i.e. it can be sued for damages by employers who suffer economic and other loss in consequence.

4.08 THE CROWN

The expression 'The Crown' refers not only to the Sovereign, who in her personal capacity is above the law, but also to all the government departments. The wide immunity formerly enjoyed by the Crown (i.e. the Government departments) was greatly restricted by the **Crown Proceedings Act 1947**. The result is that the Crown is liable in contract and in tort as occupier of premises and as an employer. However, vestiges of the former immunity remain: a judgment of a court cannot be enforced against the Crown. There is thus no question of sending in the bailiffs or seizing the property of the Crown. However, in practice the Crown complies with the declaratory judgment of the court.

SUMMARY AND DIAGRAMS

NATURAL PERSONS

Individuals

Special Categories: Minors
The mentally ill

Unincorporated Associations

Types: Clubs
Societies
Partnerships
Lloyd's Underwriters
Trade Unions

ARTIFICIAL PERSONS

Corporations

Types of Corporations: Sole
Aggregate

Types of Corporations: Aggregate
Chartered
Statutory
Registered under Companies Acts

N.B. Ultra Vires Rule

CHAPTER 5.

THE LAW OF CONTRACT

CONTRACT

5.01 **DEFINITION** — A contract is a legally binding agreement. It is made when an offer is unconditionally accepted.

5.02 **OFFER** — An offer is a firm proposal from one person, called the **offeror,** to another person called the **offeree.** It should be distinguished from the following:-

(a) **An invitation to treat.**

The purpose of an invitation to treat is to stimulate interest so that someone responds by making an offer. Examples are the display of goods in any part of a shop, most advertisements and a company prospectus. N.B. the following cases:-

Pharmaceutical Society of Great Britain -v- Boots Cash Chemists (Southern) Ltd (1953) in which a customer in a self-service store took an item from the shelves and then paid for it at the check-out. The question was whether the sale took place when the item was taken from the shelf or at the check-out. It was held that the customer made an offer to buy at the check-out which was accepted on behalf of the shop by the cashier. Thus the contract of sale was made at the check-out.

Fisher -v- Bell (1961) in which a flick-knife was displayed with a price label in a shop window. The question was whether the shop was offering it for sale by displaying it. It was held that the display was merely an invitation to treat, not an offer.

British Car Auctions -v- Wright (1972) in which an unroadworthy car was put up for auction. The question was whether the auctioneers were offering it for sale and thus committing a criminal offence. It was held that its inclusion in the auction was a mere invitation to treat, that the buyer made the offer by bidding and the auctioneers accepted that offer, i.e. the bid, by bringing down the hammer. Thus no offence had been committed by the auctioneers.

(b) **A declaration of intention**

This is a general announcement by a person that he intends to do something, e.g. hold an auction. This is not an offer and therefore it cannot be accepted.

N.B. the case of **Harris -v- Nickerson** (1873) in which a man claimed his expenses for attending an auction from which the furniture that he wished to buy had been withdrawn. His claim failed as there was no contract between him and the auctioneer.

(c) **A request for a supply of information**

Thus if one says to a shopkeeper: "How much is that diamond tiara in the window?" and the shopkeeper replies "£1000", there is a request for and a supply of information, not an offer and an acceptance.

N.B. the case of **Harvey -v- Facey** (1893) in which Mr. Harvey wanted to buy a farm called Bumper Hall Pen. He telegraphed to Mr. Facey: "Will you sell us Bumper Hall Pen? Telegraph lowest cash price." Mr. Facey telegraphed back: "Lowest price for Bumper Hall Pen £900." Mr Harvey then telegraphed: "We agree to buy Bumper Hall Pen for £900 asked by you. Please send title deeds." The Privy Council decided that there was simply a request for and supply of information and therefore no contract existed.

An offer must be communicated to the offeree before it can be converted into a contract by acceptance. This is a rule of common sense: it is obvious that no one can accept an offer of which he is ignorant. Thus if a reward is offered for the return of a lost dog and someone returns the dog in ignorance of the offer, he cannot claim the reward. If he had known of the offer, then he would have accepted by conduct, i.e. by returning the dog. An offer can be made either to a named person or persons or to a class of persons or to anyone. The latter is an offer to the whole world, as in the case of **Carlill -v- Carbolic Smoke Ball Company** (1893).

5.03 TERMINATION OF AN OFFER

Lapse — An offer does not remain open forever. If a time limit for acceptance is stipulated in the offer, then the offer must be accepted within that time. If there is no time limit, the offer must be accepted within a reasonable time. What is 'reasonable' will depend upon the circumstances. An offer to sell a consignment of ripe strawberries must obviously be accepted with speed. An offer of accommodation from a hotel should be accepted within perhaps a fortnight, unless the circumstances indicate urgency, e.g. it is high season or there is a festival in the town.

N.B. the case of **Ramsgate Victorial Hotel Co -v- Montefiore** (1866) in which a person offered to buy shares in the company in June and the company accepted the offer by allotting the shares in November of the same year (i.e. at an interval of some five months). It was held that the offer had not been accepted within a reasonable time: it had lapsed and was therefore no longer capable of acceptance.

Revocation — With certain exceptions, an offer can be revoked or withdrawn by the offeror at any time before acceptance. Thus the offeror is free to change his mind and cancel his offer but he must communicate this fact either personally or through some reliable third party to the offeree. If the offeree has not been informed of the cancellation and accepts the offer, a contract will result.

N.B. the case of **Dickinson -v- Dodds** (1876) in which a vendor offered to sell his house to a potential purchaser and to hold the offer open for a certain period but changed his mind and revoked his offer by selling to someone else. A friend of the seller, called Mr. Berry, told the offeree (i.e. the first potential buyer) of this sale. The offeree then tried to accept the offer. It was held that the revocation had been effectively communicated to the offeree and therefore no acceptance thereafter could be made. If there had been no effective communication or revocation, then there would have been a contract and consequently a breach by reason of the second sale.

Rejection and counter offer — An offer will come to an end if it is rejected. It will also come to an end if it is met by a counter-offer as this is tantamount to rejection. If I offer you my car for £1000 and you say, "I'll give you £950 for it," you are making a counter-offer. The effect is to cancel out my original offer. I can therefore either accept or reject your new offer of £950. If I reject it, you cannot insist that I sell to you at the original price of £1000. If you say, "Very well, I'll pay £1000," you are making yet another offer to which I can respond as I please. A counter-offer often takes the form of a qualified acceptance, i.e. the introduction of a proviso into the acceptance. For example, I offer you my car for £1000 and you say that you will buy it provided that I get my garage to service it first. In reality, you are not accepting my offer, you are making an offer of your own which, of course, I can accept or reject.

N.B. the case of **Hyde -v- Wrench** (1840) in which the owner of a farm offered to sell it for £1000. The offeree in turn offered £950 which was rejected. The offeree then attempted to return to the price of £1000, but this too was rejected. It was held that there was no contract.

Death — The death of the offeree will bring the offer to an end. The death of the offeror terminates the offer where there is a personal element in the offer, e.g. to sing or dance, and where the offeree knows of the death.

An offer will, of course, come to an end by acceptance as it merges with (i.e. disappears into) the agreement.

Some special cases

Options — If an offeror agrees to keep his offer open for a certain period in return for some form of consideration, e.g. a payment, he creates an option in favour of the offeree. The offeree therefore has the right to exercise the option within the specified period. A revocation of the offer would amount to a breach of a collateral contract, i.e. of a contract preliminary to the one envisaged by the option.

Tenders

An advertisement inviting tenders, e.g. for building word, is an invitation to treat. The tender (often made on the advertiser's own standard form) is an offer. It will, of course, become a contract by acceptance.

5.04 ACCEPTANCE

The basic rule is that acceptance must be communicated to the offeror. However, there are the following **two exceptions** to this rule:-

(a) **Where the offeror dispenses with the need for acceptance to be communicated,** e.g. where he offers a reward for the return of something lost. The offeror clearly envisages that acceptance may be by conduct, i.e. by the return of the thing. It should be noted, however, that the offeror cannot simply choose to interpret the offeree's silence as signifying acceptance: he cannot say, "If I hear nothing from you, I will take it that you have accepted my offer and will send you an invoice."

This situation is entirely different from the offeree accepting of his own volition by a positive act.

N.B. the case of **Felthouse -v- Bindley** (1863) in which an uncle wrote to his nephew offering to buy a horse and stating, "If I hear no more about him I consider the horse mine at £30.75". The nephew had sent the horse together with others in auction. He told the auctioneer to withdraw the horse, but the auctioneer sold it by mistake. The uncle sued the auctioneer in the tort of conversion, i.e. for wrongfully selling property belonging to him. This action failed as the court held that there was no contract between the uncle and nephew as there had been no communication of acceptance.

(b) **Where the postal rule applies.** The rule is that acceptance is effective and therefore the contract comes into existence at the moment of posting of the letter of acceptance. The rule applies where the parties must have intended the use of the post to communicate acceptance, e.g. where the offer is made by letter. The rule would not, of course, apply if the letter is not properly stamped or addressed or not properly posted, e.g. handed to the postman instead of being placed in the letter box or handed across a post office counter. It is, of course, advisable for a person posting a letter of acceptance to obtain a certificate of posting in order to prove the fact of posting. The rule was established in the cases of **Adams -v- Lindsell** (1818) and **Household Fire Insurance Co -v- Grant** (1879). In the latter case, Mr. Grant applied for shares in the company and a letter of allotment (i.e. an acceptance) was posted to him, but it did not reach him. It was held that the contract was made at the moment of posting of the acceptance.

It is important to note the operation of the postal rule in cases where the offeror attempts to withdraw his offer. It will be recalled that revocation of an offer is effective only when communicated. Thus let us suppose the following:

(a) A hotelier sends a letter offering accommodation to Mr. Bennett on 1st February.

(b) Mr. Bennett receives this offer on 2nd February and immediately posts an acceptance.

(c) The hotelier posts a letter cancelling his offer on 2nd February which reaches Mr. Bennett on 3rd February.

There is a contract between the hotelier and Mr. Bennett which was made at the moment of posting of Mr. Bennett's letter of acceptance on 2nd February. Therefore the hotelier's second letter arrives too late. If the hotelier cannot provide the accommodation he is in breach of contract.

N.B. the case of **Henthorne -v- Fraser** (1892) in which the offeree posted a letter of acceptance at 3.30 p.m. and the offeror posted a letter or revocation which reached the offeree at 5.30 p.m. the same day. It was held that there was a contract which had come into existence at 3.30 p.m. Therefore the letter of revocation, which, of course, could only be effective on arrival, was two hours too late.

It will be readily appreciated that the postal rule can create uncertainty and difficulty for a businessman who is an offeror because there will be a time when he is unaware that he is bound by a contract. There is no problem if he still has the goods which he offered for sale or the room which he offered to let. However, he may no longer have the subject matter of the proposed contract when the acceptance reaches him. He can, of course, prevent this situation arising by making it clear in his offer that an acceptance must actually be received. The postal rule will not then apply.

N.B. the case of **Holwell Securities -v- Hughes** (1974) in which it was held that the fact that an option was to be exercised by 'notice in writing to' the owner was sufficient to displace the postal rule, i.e. it was necessary for the notice which constituted the acceptance to reach the offeror, i.e. the person who had granted the option.

Instantaneous Forms of Communication.

Clearly, the postal rule does not apply to telephone conversations. If the offeror does not hear the offeree's acceptance because the line goes 'dead', there is no contract.

With regard to telex, this may or may not be a form of instantaneous communication depending, e.g. on whether it is transmitted during office hours or at night or via a third party's machine. It is clear from the cases of **Entores -v- Miles Far Eastern Corporation** (1955) and the recent House of Lord's case of **Brinkibon Ltd -v- Stahag Stahl and Stahlwarenhandelsgesellschaft GmbH** (1982) that there is no definite rule applicable in all circumstances that the contract is made where the telex acceptance is received.

Revocation of acceptance

In spite of the postal rule, it may be held that an acceptance can be effectively revoked provided that the offeror is informed of the revocation before he receives the acceptance or together with the acceptance.

N.B. the Scottish case of **Dunmore -v- Alexander** (1830) in which an offeree's letter accepting an offer of employment was followed by a letter cancelling that acceptance. Both letters reached the offeror by the same post. It was held that there was an effective cancellation of the acceptance.

'Subject to Change'

An acceptance 'subject to contract' means that a contract does not come into existence until a formal document has been drawn up and signed by both parties. Agreement to buy and sell land are invariably expressed to be 'subject to contract' and will remain so whilst searches are carried out and financial arrangements are made and until the Solicitors to the respective parties make a formal exchange of contracts.

5.05 INTENTION TO CREATE LEGAL RELATIONS

Even where there is a clear acceptance of an offer, there may be no contract because the parties do not intend to enter into a legal relationship. If you were to invite some friends to dinner and then spend many hours over a hot stove producing gastronomic delights, could you sue your friends if they failed to turn up? No doubt your instincts prompt you to say 'No'. You are correct: this was a purely social arrangement giving rise to no legal obligations.

There is a presumption that there is no intention to create legal relations in social and domestic agreements.

N.B. the case of **Balfour -v- Balfour** (1919) in which a husband agreed to make periodic payments to his wife whilst he was abroad. He failed to honour his promise and she sued him for arrears. Her claim failed as there was a presumption that an agreement between husband and wife (i.e. during the subsistence of the marriage) was not intended to be legally binding. If the parties had separated with a view to ending their marriage then the presumption would have been rebutted. Thus the case of **Merritt -v- Merritt** should be contrasted with **Balfour -v- Balfour.**

A case in which the presumption was rebutted by evidence of the parties' true intentions is **Simpkins -v- Pays** (1955) in which grandmother, granddaughter and the lodger agreed to share the cost of entering a competition in a newspaper and any winnings. They won. The lodger had to sue for his share of the winnings and his claim succeeded.

There is a presumption in commercial or business agreements that there is an intention to create legal relations. However, this presumption can be rebutted by an express statement that there is no such intention. Thus in the case of **Jones -v- Vernons Pools Ltd** (1938) the court gave effect to the statement on the football-pools coupon that the entry "shall not give rise to any legal relationships, or be legally enforceable, but bindings in honour only". This meant that a person who claimed to have won could not sue on his claim. **The general rule is that contracts can be made in any form,** i.e. orally, in writing or even by conduct. An example of the latter would be a 'silent' purchase in a supermarket. The customer takes the goods to the checkout, the assistant takes the money and the customer departs. This is not very polite, but there is a contract created by conduct!

Exceptionally, some contracts must be made in writing, e.g. hire-purchase contracts and contracts of marine insurance.

There are other types of contract which must be 'evidenced in writing'. These include contracts for the sale of land and contracts of guarantee. The word 'land' automatically includes any buildings erected on it. If there is no written evidence of these contracts, they are unenforceable by action in the courts, i.e. the contract is valid (thus a deposit could be forfeited in the event of breach) but neither party can sue to enforce his rights.

In order for a contract for the sale of land to be enforceable, there must be a 'note or memorandum' which satisfies the requirements of the **Law of Property Act 1925 S.40:-**

(i) It must identify the parties
(ii) It must identify the subject-matter of the contract.
(iii) It must state the price and any other material terms.
(iv) It must be signed by the party against whom the action is to be brought, i.e. the defendant.

The 'note' need not be in existence at the time that the contract is made, but it must be in existence by the time that court action is commenced.

However, equity will not allow a person to rely upon the requirements of the section in order to perpetrate a fraud. Thus equity has developed the doctrine of **part performance:** if the oral contract has been partly performed, then equity will enforce it by granting a decree of **specific performance.** The act of part performance must be such that it can only be understood in relation to the alleged contract, e.g. a builder orally agrees to sell a house to a family for £30,000. They pay him and he gives them the key. They take possession. Later he refuses to complete the sale by executing a conveyance in their favour. Equity would order the builder to complete the sale as the payment of so large a sum and the handing over of the key can only be explained by reference to the alleged contract.

N.B. the case of **Rawlinson -v- Ames** (1925) in which T agreed to take the lease of a flat from L. It was agreed that certain alterations should be carried out to the flat. They were done by L under the supervision of T. When the flat was ready, T then refused to sign a lease. It was held that T must sign a lease and an order for specific performance was made.

5.06 CONTRACTS UNDER SEAL

The forms of contract mentioned above are simple contracts. The word simple does not mean 'not complex' in this context, it means 'not under seal' or 'not a speciality contract'. A contract made under seal is one in the form of a deed. It differs from a simple contract in that it must comply with certain formal requirements, i.e. a person signs a deed alongside a red seal, places his finger on the seal and says 'I deliver this as my act and deed'. A deed is required for certain types of contract, e.g. to transfer the legal estate in land and to transfer a ship or a share in a ship. There are certain technical points to note, e.g. a deed often requires stamping; a simple contract followed by a deed merges into the deed unless it is stated in the contract that it shall not merge (merger has the effect that it is no longer possible to sue on the simple contract); the period during which it is possible to sue on a speciality contract is twelve years; whereas the period for a simple contract is six years; a deed is conclusive evidence of the truth of its statements, whereas a simple contract is only presumptive evidence. Consideration is not required for a deed whereas it is essential for a simple contract.

5.07 CONSIDERATION

Consideration is the promise to give or the giving of something of value. Both parties to a simple contract must give consideration. In practice, consideration commonly takes one of the following forms:-

(a) a promise to pay for goods in return for a promise to supply them;
(b) a promise to pay for a service in return for a promise to provide it.

Less common forms of consideration are better or the rendering of a service for a service. A promise to forego one's rights, e.g. not to sue can also amount to consideration.

The following rules should be noted:-

1. **Consideration need not be adequate, but must be real or genuine.** This means that the law is not concerned with the question whether a party is selling at too low a price or buying at too high a price. Thus, unless there is fraud the courts will not concern themselves with value. However, consideration must be such that it is possible to ascribe a real monetary value to it. Therefore a promise not to complain would not amount to consideration as in **White -v- Bluett** (1863).
2. **Consideration must not be past.** There must be a promise in return for a promise. Thus if your neighbour cleans your windows whilst you are on holiday without having been asked to do so and you promise to pay him on your return, your promise is unenforceable as the consideration which he gave for it was already past, i.e. he had done the work at the time that you made your promise. There is no contract between you. In **Re: McArdle** (1951) the occupants of a house carried out repairs. The owners then agreed in writing to pay for them. The occupants' claim to enforce this promise failed.

   This situation should be contrasted with a request for work to be done, but without mention of payment. There will then be an implied promise to pay a reasonable sum at the time of the request and the sum will simply be quantified after the work is completed. There is therefore good consideration. For example, you ask a plumber to stop a leaking tap. He does so and you then agree a price. You are, of course, obliged to pay because the very fact of requesting him to do the work carries an implied promise to pay.

3. **A promise to perform an existing obligation does not amount to consideration.** Thus if a bank manager says to a clerk, "I will pay you an extra £5 if you will count those bank notes," and the clerk does so and claims the promised £5, the claim will not succeed. The reason is that the clerk is merely doing his job for which he is already receiving a salary. If, however, the bank manager says to a girl clerk, "Arrest that masked robber and I will pay you £100", the girl who leaps the counter and pins the raider to the floor and then demands the £100 will succeed in her claim. She has acted beyond the call of duty and has therefore given consideration for the promise to pay extra.
4. Consideration must **move from the promisee.** The promisee is the person to whom the promise is made. The promisor is the person who makes the promise. The above statement means that the promisee himself (and not some other person) must provide the consideration. In other words, this is one way of expressing the **privity of contract rule,** i.e. only a party to a contract can sue on it. Thus if Jack instructs the florist to send flowers to Jill and the flowers are dying when they reach her, only Jack can sue the florist because he is the party on the contract, i.e. he gave consideration to the florist in agreeing to pay for the flowers. Thus a stranger to a contract cannot rely upon its provisions or sue on it as was made clear by the House of Lords in **Scruttons Ltd -v- Midland Silicones Ltd** (1962).
5. Consideration must, of course, be legal, e.g. not a promise to commit an offence.

   It should be noted that consideration starts as being **executory** and ends as being **executed.** Executory consideration is a promise to do something, e.g. to pay; executed consideration is the fulfillment of the promise, i.e. the payment.

5.08 THE DOCTRINE OF ESTOPPEL

This is an equitable doctrine and is expounded in the Court of Appeal case of **Central London Property Trust Ltd -v- High Trees House Ltd** (1947) in which the owner of a block of flats agreed to reduce rent because the tenant was unable to sublet all the flats on account of war-time conditions. When the war ended, the owner claimed arrears of rent. His claim failed as the tenant had relied upon the waiver by the owner of his full legal rights, i.e. his entitlement to the full rent. The tenant had given no consideration for the reduction in rent, but nevertheless equity kept the owner to his word as regards the past (i.e. the period prior to 1945). The owner could, of course, insist upon the full rent for the future in view of the absence of consideration. Thus a party who makes a waiver of his rights on which the other relies, i.e. acts may be estopped from insisting on his full rights even though consideration is absent.

5.09 TERMS OF THE CONTRACT

An offer should contain all the terms and the contract. There may, of course, be considerable period of negotiation before terms are agreed and a final offer emerges and is accepted.

There are two types of term: an **express term,** i.e. one that is actually mentioned, e.g. the price of goods: and an **implied term,** i.e. one that is present even though it is not mentioned, e.g. a term that work will be carried out with reasonable care and skill.

5.10 EXPRESS TERMS

The basic rule is that all terms must be made known to the other party before the contract is made. Where terms are contained in some document, e.g. British Rail's terms of carriage, they must be effectively incorporated into the contract.

There is a group of cases known as 'the ticket cases' which developed these principles, e.g. **Henderson -v- Stevenson** (1875) in which a steamer ticket stated on the front or face 'Dublin to Whitehaven'. In fact there was a clause excluding the steamship company's liability for loss or damage. It was held that a passenger was not bound by the clause because it had not been drawn to his attention. On the other hand, in **Penton -v- Southern Railway Co** (1931) a ticket stated on the face of it: "For conditions see back". It was held that the conditions were effectively incorporated. It is, of course, no valid excuse that the other party fails to read what was readily accessible to him.

The following case illustrate the same principles:-

Olley -v- Marlborough Court Ltd (1949) in which a lady booked into the company's hotel in reception and was shown directly to her room. On the wall was a notice to the effect that the management accepted no responsibility for loss of or damage to a guest's possessions unless they were deposited for safe custody. The lady's fur coat was stolen. The company sought to rely upon the notice. It was held that they could not do so as it was seen, and could only be seen, **after** the contract had been made in reception. However, if there had been a 'course of dealing' between the parties, i.e. the lady had stayed at that hotel on many previous occasions and was aware of the notice, the result of the case could have been different.

Thornton -v- Shoe Lane Parking Co Ltd (1971) in which Mr. Thornton drove to the barrier of a multi-storey car park, took a ticket and entered when the light showed green. The ticket referred to conditions displayed inside the premises. These conditions included an exclusion clause. An accident due to the Company's negligence occurred when Mr. Thornton went to collect his car and the Company sought to rely upon the exclusion clause. It was held that they could not do so as the exclusion clause had not been effectively drawn to Mr. Thornton's attention before the contract was made. In particular, Mr. Thornton was 'on risk' the moment he had passed the barrier.

Thus an insurance company must do everything reasonable to bring its terms to the attention of the proposer, i.e. the person applying for insurance cover. If it has done so, the insured will be bound even though he has not read the terms. There is authority in the Court of Appeal case of **General Accident Insurance Corporation -v- Cronk** (1901) that only the principal terms need be made knwon to the proposer, i.e. premium, commencement of cover, duration of cover, the risk covered.

It should be noted that express written terms can be varied orally as in **Curtis -v- Chemical Cleaning and Dyeing Co Ltd** (1951) in which a lady took a wedding dress to the cleaners and was asked to sign a document. In response to her enquiry as to the effect of the document, the assistant replied that it protected the company from liability for damage to sequins and beads. In reality, it protected the company from all liability. When the dress was damaged and the lady claimed, the company sought to rely upon its exclusion clause. It was held that they could not do so as the assistant had apparent authority to vary the clause and she had done so.

Similarly, an express oral promise given when a contract is made will override an inconsistent written term as in **Mendelsohn -v- Normand Ltd** (1970) in which a garage attendant promised a car owner that he would lock his car after moving it as the owner had told him that it contained valuable property. The attendant handed the owner a ticket which stated that the garage accepted no responsibility for loss of the contents of a car. The contents were stolen. It was held that the company was liable as their attendant had apparent authority to give an assurance about the safety of a car and its contents.

5.11 IMPLIED TERMS

These can be implied by the **custom** of a trade, **law**, or by **statute.** Examples of terms implied at common law are that a hotel room will be reasonably fit for human habitation; that a house will be built in a good and workmanlike manner with proper materials.

Examples of terms implied by statute are those contained in sections 12 to 15 of the **Sale of Goods Act 1979.** Briefly, S12 implies a condition that the seller has the right to sell the goods; S.13 implies a condition that the goods will correspond with any description; S.14 implies a condition where the sale is made in the course of a business that the goods will be of merchantable quality, i.e. reasonably fit for the purpose for which they are sold.

5.12 UNFAIR CONTRACT TERMS ACT 1977

The effect of this statute is to limit the freedom of the parties to insert into a contract whatever terms they please. In practice, this means that the freedom of the stronger party to exclude his liability in some situations is restricted. Thus where a business is dealing with a consumer or on its own written standard terms of contract, it cannot exclude or restrict its liability for breach of contract save in so far as its exclusion (or exemption) clause satisfies the test of reasonableness laid down in S.11 of the Act. Also, in either of these circumstances, the business cannot vary the terms of the contract in accordance with a variation clause unless the clause passes the reasonableness test. An example of the latter types of clause would be one where the business stated, "the company reserves the right to substitute a different hotel to the one chosen."

The consumer's 'statutory rights', i.e. the buyer's rights under S.12-15 of the **Sale of Goods Act** (1979) and corresponding provision in favour of the consumer in other statutes, cannot be excluded in any circumstances. Attempts to deprive the trade purchaser of corresponding rights are subject to the reasonableness test.

A business can no longer exclude liability for causing death or personal injury through negligence. An attempt to exclude liability for causing other types of loss is subject to the reasonableness test.

Finally, it should be noted the party who seeks to rely upon an exclusion clause which is subject to the reasonableness test, must prove that it passes the test.

UNFAIR CONTRACT TERMS ACT 1977

Exclusion Clauses in Business Contracts — The requirement of reasonableness

Guidelines for the application of the requirement of reasonableness are provided in Schedule 2 to the 1977 Act. The guidelines state that regard shall be had to any of the following:

(a) The relative strength of the bargaining positions of the parties, taking into account alternative means by which the customer's requirements could have been met;
(b) whether the customer received any inducement to agree to the exclusion clause or had an opportunity of entering a similar contract with other persons without having to agree to a similar clause;
(c) whether the customer knew, or ought reasonably to have known, of the clause;
(d) where the clause excludes or restricts a liability if some condition is not complied with, whether it was reasonable at the time of the contract to expect that compliance with that condition would be practicable; or
(e) whether the goods were manufactured, processed or adapted to the special order of the customer.

Standard terms of business and guarantees

Where one of the parties deals as a consumer or on the other's written standard terms of business, the other cannot by reference to any contract term:

(a) when himself in breach of contract, exclude or restrict any liability of his in respect of the breach; or

(b) claim to be entitled —

(i) to render a contractual performance substantially different from that which was reasonably expected of him, or

(ii) in respect of the whole or any part of his contractual obligations, to render no performance at all.

Cases on the requirement of reasonableness include **George Mitchell -v- Finney Lock Seeds** (1983) and **Ailsa Craig Fishing Co -v- Malvern Fishing Co** (1983). Note also the following:

HUGHES -v- HALL (1981)
"sold as seen and inspected" — trying to exclude description of car which was incorrect. Criminal case.

CAVENDISH WOODHOUSE -v- MARLEY (1984)
"bought as seen" means no sale by description therefore no breach. (Furniture).

PHILLIPS PRODUCTS -v- HYLAND (1985)
Plant hire with driver. Contract said driver was hirer's responsibility. Held valid exclusion clause.

WOODMAN -v- PHOTOTRADE PROCESSING (1981)
Clause "All photographic materials are accepted on the basis that their value does not exceed the loss of the material itself. Responsibility is limited to the replacement of the film. No liability will be accepted, consequential or otherwise, however caused". Film of special value — wedding photographs — only ones taken. Exclusion clause standard throughout trade therefore consumer no real choice. Dixons could foresee film may be irreplaceable therefore exclusion clause unreasonable and £75 compensation granted.

INTERFOTO v-v STILETTO (1987)
Note sent to agency requesting transparencies of 1950's. In reply agency sent 47 transparencies in a bag with written note of conditions £x for 14 days and additional charge of £5 a day for each transparency after this period. Company ran up £3000 bill (13 days) **Held** no reasonable attention drawn to clause — the more severe the clause the greater the attention must be drawn to it.

5.13 CAPACITY TO CONTRACT

A party to a contract must have the legal capacity to enter into that contract. Adult natural persons, i.e. those not suffering under a legal disability such as mental ill health have full contractural capacity. Corporations can only make contracts which are within the scope of the objects clause of the Memorandum of Association. If they act outside their powers, they are said to act 'ultra vires'.

Minors

Minors, also referred to as infants, are persons aged under eighteen years. The law relating to minors is found in the **Minors Contracts Act 1987.**

Valid Contracts

Minors are bound by two types of contract; **a contract for the purchase of necessaries** and **a contract of service or education.** Necessaries are goods (or services) which are needed by the minor both at the time that they are ordered and at the time of delivery (or performance of the service) and are suitable for the minor's condition or status in life. Thus a minor can always cancel an executory contract, i.e. before the delivery of the necessaries. A wealthy minor will be liable on a greater range of contracts than a poor one.

N.B. the case of **Nash -v- Inman** (1908) in which a Cambridge undergraduate ordered and received eleven fancy waistcoats from a Savile Row tailor. The tailor sued for payment, but the claim failed as it was shown that the undergraduate was already well supplied with clothes.

Even when the goods do rank as necessaries, the minor is only liable to pay a 'reasonable sum' for them, a trader would therefore be well advised to demand payment in advance, the minor cannot reclaim money paid to the trader unless there has been a complete failure of consideration.

A minor is bound by a contract of service, i.e. of employment if, taken as a whole it is for his benefit. A contract for a child 'star' actress is unlikely to be binding, even though it might be lucrative, as the style of life might disrupt the child's education and adversely affect her health. It is not necessary that every single term of the contract should be beneficial as is shown by **Doyle -v- White City Stadium Ltd** (1935) in which it was held that the infant boxer was bound by the terms of a licence issued by the Boxing Board of Control even though one term stipulated that his money would be stopped if he was disqualified.

Void Contracts

The following types of contract are void, i.e. the minor cannot be sued upon them:- trading contracts, i.e. those where the minor is in business on his own account and fails, e.g. to deliver goods or perform a service; contracts of loan; contracts for the purchase of goods which are not necessaries, e.g. mere luxuries; accounts stated.

The effect of a void contract is that the adult cannot, of course, sue for breach of contract; moreover, he cannot sue in the tort of deceit as that would be an indirect way of enforcing the contract. However, equity can order the minor to return the goods provided that two conditions are fulfilled:

(i) the minor has obtained the goods by fraud, e.g. by lying about his age; and,

(ii) the minor still has the exact goods in his possession.

It should be noted that a minor is fully liable in the criminal law if he obtains goods by deception; he can, therefore, face prosecution.

Voidable Contracts

These are contracts which are binding on a minor unless and until he repudiates them either during minority or within a reasonable time thereafter. They are contracts which entail a continuing obligation, e.g. contracts of partnership; the holding of shares in a company; the holding of a lease of a property.

Mentally Ill and Drunken Persons

If the other party to the contract knows of the insanity or drunkenness, as the case may be, the contract is voidable at the option of the insane or drunken person.

The burden of proving the fact lies on the party seeking avoidance of the contract. However, mentally ill persons and drunken persons are liable for necessaries in the same way that minors are liable.

5.14 LEGALITY

Obviously a contract which is illegal will not be upheld by the courts. Thus a contract to commit a crime, e.g. to murder someone or defraud the Inland Revenue cannot be enforced through the courts. Therefore, if a client and a builder agree that a certain sum shall not 'pass through the books' in order to avoid tax, the client loses his right to sue the builder for shoddy work. Sometimes a contract can be performed in a legal way or an illegal way. It is obviously not illegal to hire a vehicle, but the vehicle could be used for an illegal or immoral purpose. In the case of **Pearce -v- Brooks** (1866), a prostitute hired a carriage for the purpose of soliciting men. This fact was known to the owners of the carriage and their claim for the hire-charge failed. Had they not known of the purpose for which the carriage was required, their claim would doubtless have succeeded.

Contracts in restraint of trade, e.g. imposed on the sale of a business or on employees to prevent them from competing with their employer after leaving his service are void unless they are (a) not contrary to the public interest and (b) fair and reasonable as between the parties. This means that the restraint must be no greater than is required to protect the interests of the purchaser of a business or the goodwill and trade secrets of the employer whose employee is leaving his service. Thus the restraint must not be of too long duration or relate to too wide an area. In **Mason -v- Provident Clothing Co Ltd** (1913), the House of Lords decided that a clause restraining a clothing company's canvasser from working in a similar job within 25 miles of London for 3 years was void as being wider than was required to protect the employers' interests. Where a contract contains a reasonable restraint and a void one, the latter can be severed so that the reasonable one still stands.

5.15 MISREPRESENTATION

A misrepresentation is **an incorrect statement of material fact.** It is made before a contract by one party to another in order to **induce** that other into entering into the contract and the other does so in reliance upon the statement and suffers loss as a result.

The statement must be a statement of **fact,** not of law, but an opinion, especially one given by an expert, may imply knowledge of facts upon which it is based. Thus if a motor dealer describes a car as being in "excellent mechanical order" and it proves to be defective, he may be liable as he will be taken to have factual grounds for his opinion.

An example of statements which commonly induce contracts are those contained in travel brochures. If a hotel is said to be "five minutes walking distance from the beach" and in reality it is half an hour away, there will be a misrepresentation. However, it must be clear that the other person entered into the contract on the strength of the statement. If he in fact relied either on his own judgment or that of a third party, his claim will fail. If the purchaser of a house instructs a surveyor to survey it, he cannot claim to have relied upon statements made by the vendor as to its condition.

If circumstances change between the making of the statement and the making of the contract, the maker of the statement is under a duty to correct it so as to reflect the change. In **With -v- O'Flanagan** (1936) a doctor stated that his practice was producing an income of £2000 per annum. He then became ill and the takings fell considerably. He did not disclose this fact to his purchaser and the purchaser succeeded in obtaining rescission of the contract.

5.16 Types of Misrepresentation

1. **Fraudulent misrepresentation:** this is a statement known to be false by the marker, i.e. a lie, or one made recklessly, i.e. without the maker caring whether it be true or false. As the same facts would normally also amount to a criminal offence, the standard of proof is 'beyond reasonable doubt'.

   N.B. the case of **Edgington -v- Fitzmaurice** (1885) in which it was stated in a company prospectus that money was required to finance expansion. The plaintiff advanced money on the strength of this statement which was in fact used to pay off existing debts. It was held that there there was a fraudulent misrepresentation of intention.
2. **Negligent misrepresentation:** this consists of a failure to take reasonable care in circumstances where the law imposes a duty of care. The leading case is **Hedley Byrne -v- Heller and Partners Ltd** (1964) and this will be dealt with under the heading of "Torts".
3. **Innocent misrepresentation** is any misrepresentation which is neither fraudulent nor negligent is innocent.

Remedies for misrepresentation

The remedies available to the innocent party, i.e. the party misled are as follows:-

1. He can refuse further performance of the contract upon discovering the misrepresentation, e.g. he can refuse to pay.
2. If the misrepresentation is **fraudulent,** he can request the court to rescind the contract and claim an award of damages based on the tort of deceit.
3. If the misrepresentation is **negligent,** he can request rescission and claim an award of damages based on the rule in the case of **Hedley Byrne -v- Heller and Parnters Ltd** or under the **Misrepresentation Act 1967 S.2(i).**
4. If the misrepresentation is **innocent,** he can request rescission and/or claim damages under S.2 of the 1967 Act. It should be noted that damages for this kind of misrepresentation are discretionary under the Act (unlike common law damages which are awarded as of right). Moreover, the court may award damages in lieu of rescission where it considers it equitable to do so. Finally, the party misled can, of course, affirm, i.e. go ahead with, the contract if he so wishes.

   Any attempt by one party to exclude liability for misrepresentation is subject to the reasonableness test. Moreover, it is for the party seeking to rely on the exclusion clause to prove that it is reasonable.

Duty of disclosure

There is normally no duty to disclose material facts in the course of negotiations leading to a contract. Even so a party must be careful to avoid half-truths which distort the true picture.

Exceptionally, there is a duty of disclosure in contracts classified as **'uberrimae fidei'.** The most important type of contract of this nature is, of course, a contract of insurance. The proposer must declare all material facts, i.e. facts which would influence a prudent insurer in deciding whether to accept the risk and, if so, at what premium. A failure to make full disclosure renders the contract **voidable** at the option of the insurers, i.e. it is up to them whether they choose to repudiate the contract.

5.17 MISTAKE

A mistake of law has no effect upon the validity of a contract as 'ignorance of the law is no excuse'.

The general rule is that mistakes of fact also have no effect upon validity, but there are important exceptions to this rule. Firstly, it should be noted that private misunderstandings by one party do not vitiate the contract. If Mr. Thorpe goes into an antique shop and says, "I'll have that cigarette case, please", as he thinks that it is solid silver whereas it is, in fact, only silver plate, he cannot demand his money back when he realises his mistake. We are, of course, assuming that there is no misrepresentation by the seller. If the law were otherwise, a person could always claim to be the victim of his own mistake and commercial transactions would be insecure. There is sound sense, therefore, in the **caveat emptor** rule, i.e. 'Let the buyer beware'.

The exceptions to the rule occur where there is a **fundamental mistake of material fact** which vitiates the consent of one party to the transaction. These exceptions are as follows:-

1. **Where there is a mistake made by one party of which the other party is aware** (i.e. a public mistake rather than a mere private misunderstanding) as in **Scriven Bros and Co -v- Hindley and Co.** (1913) in which the auctioneers knew that they were selling tow and the buyers thought they were buying hemp and the auctioneers must have been aware of the mistake in view of the price bid. It was held that there was no contract. Similarly, if a party makes an arithmetical error in an offer, e.g. a tender, which is apparent to the other party, there will be no contract if that offer is accepted. Thus in these instances, there is an attempt by one party to take advantage of the mistake by the other.

2. **Where there is a common mistake** (i.e. the same mistake made by both parties) with regard to the existence of the subject matter of the contract as in **Couturier -v- Hastie** (1852) in which there was an agreement for the sale of a cargo of corn.

   Unknown to both parties, the corn had begun to deteriorate and the captain of the ship had sold it under his power before the agreement was made. Therefore, in reality, there was nothing to contract about and it was held that there was no contract.

   Similarly, in **Strickland -v- Turner** (1852) there was the purchase of an annuity in respect of a person who, unknown to either party, was already dead. Again, it was held that there was no contract.

3. **Where there is a mutual mistake** regarding the subject mater of a contract, i.e. the parties are each thinking of a different thing, they are at cross purposes, or, expressed differently, they simply misunderstand each other. In **Raffles -v- Wichelhaus** (1864) there was an agreement for the sale of a cargo of cotton "Ex Peerless" sailing from Bombay. The parties did not realise that there were two ships, both called "Peerless" and both sailing from Bombay. The one ship was sailing in October, and the other in December. It was held that there was no contract as the seller was thinking of one ship and the buyer was thinking of the other ship. Hence, they had never really agreed.

4. **Where a party mistakenly signs a document and succeeds in raising the plea of 'Non est factum'**, i.e. 'it is not my act'.

   The basic rule is that a person is bound by a document which he signs whether he has bothered to read it or not. If the laws were otherwise, a party could always escape from his obligations by omitting to read a document. The plea of 'non est factum' will only succeed if both the following conditions are fulfilled:-

(i) The document is of a **fundamentally different** character to the one which he thinks he is signing as in **Foster -v- Mackinnon** (1869) in which an elderly man with poor eyesight was induced to sign a Bill of Exchange (which creates a primary liability) when he thought that he was signing a guarantee (which creates a secondary liability). It was held that he was not liable.

(ii) The person who signs must **not have been negligent.** It is for the person who signs to disprove negligence and he is more likely to succeed if he was suffering from a disability, e.g. senility or blindness and was tricked into signing, i.e. he was the victim of a fraud.

The House of Lords' decision in **Saunders -v- Anglia Building Society** (1971) shows how difficult it is for a plaintiff to succeed with the plea. An elderly lady, who had broken her spectacles, was tricked in to singing an assignment (a form of transfer) of her house to a trickster. She believed that she was executing a deed of gift in favour of her nephew. The trickster promptly mortgaged the property to the Anglia. It was held that her plea of 'non est factum' failed for she had intended to part with the ownership of her house, albeit not to the trickster. Therefore the mortgage to the Anglia was valid.

5. **Where a party is mistaken as to the identity of the other party and can prove that he regarded the identity as material.** In practice, it is very difficult for the mistaken party to prove this. There is a presumption that if A contracts with X, he intends to contract with X. It is for A to prove that he intended to contract only with B. If you go shopping, the shop-keeper does not ask your identity before he will serve you; he is happy to deal with the person who chances to be in front of him. The following cases should be compared and contrasted:-

(i) **Cundy -v- Lindsay and Co** (1878) in which a rogue called Blenkarn pretended to be Blenkiron and Co, a firm with whom the seller, Lindsay and Co, had had dealings. By this means the rogue obtained goods on credit and resold them to an innocent third party, Cundy. On the evidence, Lindsay and Co were able to prove that they intended only to sell to the reputable firm, Blenkiron and Co, and not to the rogue, Blenkarn. Therefore the contract was void and Cundy had no right to the goods even though he had no knowledge of the fraud and had paid for them.

(ii) **Phillips -v- Brooks Ltd** (1919) in which a rogue pretended to be one 'Sir George Bullough' and prevailed upon a jeweller to part with some jewels in return for a cheque which was dishonoured. The rogue then pawned the jewels and the jeweller sued the pawnbroker for their return. It was held that the contract was not void for mistake, but merely voidable for fraud. Therefore the claim against the pawnbroker failed.

(iii) **Ingram -v- Little** (1960) in which the Misses Ingram sold their car to a rogue who pretended to be P.G.M. Hutchinson, a reputable businessman. They took steps to satisfy themselves as to the buyer's identity before accepting his cheque. The rogue resold the car to an innocent third party and the cheque was dishonoured. It was held that, on the particular facts, the ladies, i.e. the sellers, had rebutted the presumption that they intended to deal simply with the person in front of them. Therefore the ladies could recover the car from the innocent third party.

(iv) **Lewis -v- Averay** (1971) in which a rogue prevailed upon the seller of a car to accept his cheque by pretending that he was Richard Greene, a well known film star. He produced a Pinewood Studios pass in support of his claim. As in the previous case, the rogue then resold the car to an innocent third party and the cheque was dishonoured. It was held that the contract was not void for material mistake of fact, but merely voidable for fraud and therefore the innocent third party could keep the car.

5.18 **Effect of Mistake**

The courts are slow to come to the conclusion that a "contract" is void for material mistake of fact (i.e. that there is no contract). The reason is apparent from the above cases: if the "contract" between A and B is void, then the next contract betwen B and C is automatically void and C will have to return the goods or to pay their value to A. However, if the contract between A and B is merely voidable for fraud, it remains valid unless and until it is rescinded, i.e. set aside. If, before rescission, there has been a resale to C, an innocent buyer, then title to i.e. ownership of, the goods passes to C and therefore C can keep the goods. Rescission is, of course, an equitable remedy, i.e. a discretionary remedy, and it will be refused by the courts if an innocent third party has acquired the goods for value, e.g. if the contract between A and B is void, the courts have no discretion; they cannot protect the innocent third party. The position may be summarised in the following diagrams:-

A B	C	X Y	Z
Sale void	Goods must be returned	Sale voidable	Goods are not returnable

5.19 **Rectification**

Rectification can be ordered by the court where a written agreement does not record the true agreement reached by the parties provided that there is evidence of the true agreement. The court will not substitute a different agreement, it merely corrects the expression used by the parties to reflect their real intention.

Finally, it should be noted that equity will sometimes rescind a contract entered into under a mistake where the common law would not regard it as void, provided that a third party has not acquired rights in the subject matter.

5.20 DURESS

Duress makes a contract voidable by the party who is the victim of it, i.e. who is the victim of violence or threats of violence.

5.21 UNDUE INFLUENCE

This is a more subtle form of coercion. It is the overbearing of the will of a weaker party by a stronger party. Again the effect is to make the contract voidable by the weaker party provided that he seeks rescission within a reasonable time.

There is a presumption of undue influence in 'fiduciary' relationships, i.e. those based upon trust, e.g. trustee and beneficiary, doctor and patient, solicitor and client, parent and child, religious advisor and disciple. This means that the stronger party must bring evidence to rebut the presumption, e.g. by showing that the weaker party received independent advice. In other cases, the weaker party must prove the undue influence. The wife succeeded in doing so in **Cresswell -v- Potter** (1978) where, in the course of divorce proceedings, she transferred her share in the matrimonial home to her husband for much less than its value. She had not received independent advice and was poorly educated. She was awarded half the proceeds of the sale of the house after the contract between her and her husband was set aside.

5.22 ASSIGNMENT

An assignment of a contract means the transfer of rights under the contract, e.g. a tenant (or lessee) who holds a 99 year lease of which 85 years remain unexpired can assign the residue of the lease. A debt due under a contract and the proceeds of a policy of life assurance can also be assigned.

Before we consider technicalities, let us look at the procedure of assigning the proceeds of a life policy. Mr. Rawlings raises a mortgage on his house with a building society and agrees to assign to the society his policy of life assurance by way of collateral security. He executes a Deed of Assignment in favour of the society and delivers it to them together with the policy and the deeds of the house. He sends a notice to the insurance company informing them of the assignment. The transaction is thus

Insurance company
i.e. the debtor

Mr. Rawlings i.e. the life
assured and assignor

Building Society
i.e. the assignee

Let us now consider the technicalities. There are two broad categories of property: **choses in possession,** i.e. things of which one can take physical possession, and **choses in action,** i.e. intangible property the right to which can only be enforced by an action in the courts.

Choses in action divide into legal choses, e.g. a debt due under a contract and equitable choses, e.g. the interest of a beneficiary under a trust fund.

There are also two forms of assignment: **legal** and **equitable.** Any chose can be assigned in either manner.

A **legal assignment** is one which satisfies the requirements of **S.136 of the Law of Property Act 1925** which are as follows:-

1) The assignment must be **in writing;**
2) It must be **signed by the assignor** (i.e. by the person making the assignment);
3) It must be **absolute** (i.e. an assignment of the whole of the debt);
4) Written **notice** of assignment must be given to the debtor.

It will be seen that our example of Mr. Rawlings' assignment of a life policy was a legal assignment.

An **equitable assignment** is one where some or all of these requirements are not satisfied. However, there must be evidence of an intention to assign. It is the practice of some building societies to take only equitable assignment of a life policy. In practice, they simply take the policy itself and deposit it with the deeds of the house which is in mortgage to them. The only memorandum in writing would be a condition on the offer of mortgage to the borrower (i.e. the life assured) that a policy should be deposited with the society. There would also normally be an undertaking by the life assured to execute a formal assignment (i.e. a legal one) if called upon to do so.

The main advantage of a legal assignment is that it enables the assignee, e.g. the building society or bank or sue the debtor to enforce the debt in its own name. In the case of an equitable assignment, the assignee often has to join the assignor as a party to the action.

The problem inherent in both types of assignment is that the assignment is 'subject to equities', i.e. to defects in title of the assignor. This means, for example, that if the life assured had failed to make a full disclosure of material facts to the insurance company at the time of making the proposal for the insurance, the policy would be voidable at the option of the insurers. The assignee of the policy, e.g. the building society or bank could be in no better position than the assignor. Therefore the insurers could refuse payment to the assignee.

Where the personality of a contracting party is important to the other, it is not possible to assign rights under the contract, e.g. under a contract of employment or a contract of motor insurance. It is also not possible to assign a right where this might increase the burden of the other party.

5.23 NOVATION

This is the name given to the transfer of obligations under a contract. If B wishes to be released from his obligations under his contract with A by substituting C, this can only be achieved with the consent of all parties, i.e. of A, B and C. Thus, if a builder finds a second builder who is willing to 'take over the contract' between himself and his client, the substitution can only take place if the client consents. Novation is in practice common, e.g. where a business takes over another business. If the customers allow their orders to be fulfilled by the new business, they are impliedly agreeing a novation.

Novation should not, however, be confused with subcontracting. This is common in the building trade and the main contractor remains liable to the client for the work of the sub-contractors. In the case of novation the first builder would be released.

5.24 DEATH AND BANKRUPTCY

When a person dies, his rights and obligations under a contract devolve upon his personal representatives by operation of law, i.e. automatically. Purely personal rights and obligations, e.g. under the deceased's contract of employment do not pass.

Similarly, the rights and obligations of a bankrupt pass to his trustee in bankruptcy, but the trustee has the right to disclaim (i.e. refuse to be bound by) onerous obligations. Again purely personal rights and obligations do not pass.

Finally, assignment should be contrasted with **negotiability.** Cheques, bills of exchange, bank notes and bankers' drafts are the best known members of a category called negotiable instruments. A person to whom such an instrument is negotiated in good faith and for value can acquire a better title than his transferor. An assignee can, of course, get no better title than his assignor. For example, a trickster manages to persuade a businessman to draw a cheque in his favour for a non-existent debt. In other words, he obtains the cheque by fraud, the trickster then indorses the cheque in favour of his garage in return for petrol. The garage knows nothing of the fraud and can sue both the trickster and the drawer of the cheque.

5.25 DISCHARGE

The principal ways in which a contract may be discharged (i.e. brought to an end) are by: **performance, frustration, agreement** and **acceptance of breach.**

Performance

This consists in the carrying out of the obligations of the contract, i.e. the performance of the service, the delivery of the goods, the tendering of payment.

With regard to time, performance must be within the time stipulated by the contract. If no time is mentioned, then performance must be within a reasonable time. Sometimes, the date for performance is either expressly or impliedly 'of the essence of the contract'. This means that the time of performance is a condition of the contract. Therefore a breach entitles the innocent party to treat the contract as repudiated by the party in default, i.e. the innocent party can refuse to perform his own obligations under the contract, for example, a hotelier orders food for a wedding reception to be held on a certain date. If the supplier fails to deliver the food on the date agreed, the hotelier can refuse to take delivery at a later date and can refuse to pay. Even if it were not expressly stated that time was 'of the essence', this would be readily understood by the parties.

Time can be made 'of the essence' by one party giving notice to that effect to the other, as in **Chas Richards Ltd -v- Oppenheim** (1950) in which Oppenheim ordered a Rolls Royce chasis and car body. The agreed delivery date was not honoured. He then wrote to the company stating that he would cancel the order if the car was not ready within four weeks. The car was not completed until some months later. Oppenheim then refused to take delivery and pay. It was held that he was entitled to do so as his notice had made time 'of the essence'. It is important, of course, that the notice should give the other party a reasonable opportunity to fulfill his obligations.

Payment

Payment must be made in legal tender unless otherwise agred with the creditor. If payment is wrongfully refused, the debtor can protect himself by making a payment into court. If payment is sent by post, the risk of loss is borne by the sender, unless the creditor has requested use of the post. Where the payment is made by negotiable instrument, e.g. a cheque, it is conditional payment only. If the cheque is dishonoured, the creditor may sue either on the debt or the cheque.

The **tender of goods** must be in accordance with the terms of the contract and give the recipient party an opportunity to see whether the goods are in accordance with the contract. Where there is a wrongful rejection of the goods tendered, the party tendering is discharged (i.e. freed from further obligation). With regard to the **standard required for performance,** the common law rule is that performance must be exact, i.e. exactly in accordance with the terms of the contract. As this rule was very harsh in practice, another doctrine was developed, that of substantial performance. This means that if a party has substantially performed his obligations, he is entitled to payment, less a reduction to reflect slight departures from the standard required by the contract.

Action by other party

Where one party **prevents performance** of the contract, e.g. by preventing a builder from getting access to the site, the other party, e.g. the builder is discharged from obligation.

Frustration

Discharge by frustration occurs where the **performance of the contract is prevented by circumstances beyond the control of either party,** e.g. a natural disaster such as an earthquake or some other supervening impossibility.

The general rule is that a contract is not discharged because one party finds it impossible to fulfill his obligations. Therefore the doctrine of frustration is an exception to this rule. There **will be no frustration** in the following circumstances:-

1) Where one party finds that he has to incur extra expense in order to perform his obligations, as in **Davis Contractors Ltd -v- Fareham UDC** (1956) in which the builders found themselves in great difficulty in fulfilling their contract to build houses for the Council due to bad weather and shortage of labour. The House of Lords held that these factors did not frustrate the contract. Such problems commonly face the building trade.
2) Strikes.
3) Non-delivery of materials to a seller so that he in turn is unable to fulfill his contractual obligations.

All of the above are the normal risks of business, the businessman should guard against them by an appropriate clause in the contract, e.g. a builder could insist upon a price variation or fluctuation, e.g. as in the Joint Contracts Tribunal (JTC) form of contract.

There **will be frustration** in the following circumstances:-

1) Where the place in which the contract was to be performed is **destroyed,** as in **Taylor -v- Caldwell** (1865) in which Caldwell let a concert hall to Taylor for a series of concerts, but it was burnt down by accident before the concerts began. It was held that the contract was frustrated.
2) Where the contract is of a **personal nature** and the party who was to render a personal service dies or is ill, as in **Robinson -v- Davison** (1871) in which a pianist was ill and unable to fulfill her contract. It was held that the contract was frustrated. If a party to such a contract is unable through illness to perform as much as is required by the contract, there may be frustration as in **Condor -v- The Barron Knights Ltd** (1966) in which the drummer fell ill and could only manage to work four nights instead of seven. Held, the contract was frustrated.
3) Where the **occurrence of a certain event** is the basis upon which the contract is made, as in **Krell -v- Henry** (1903) in which a contract was made for the hire of rooms in the Mall from which the Coronation procession of Edward VII could be viewed. The Coronation was postponed due to the illness of the King. It was held that the contract was frustrated and therefore a claim for the balance of the rent failed. However, it is a matter of fact whether the event in question was the basis of the contract and there are cases on similar facts where the decision went the opposite way.
4) Where the parties are **prevented from performing the contract by war.** If the U.K. is involved in the war, trading with the enemy becomes illegal and therefore there is immediate frustration. If the war is between foreign states, it is a matter of fact whether the war frustrates the contract: frustration will only occur when it becomes clear that performance is

impossible or would be radically different from what was reasonably contemplated by the parties at the time of making the contract — **National Carriers Ltd -v- Panalpina Ltd** (1981).

5) Where performance is rendered **illegal** through a new law, i.e. a new statute or regulation made under it, but not where the exercise of existing statutory powers interfers with performance, e.g. the exercise by a local authority of powers of compulsory purchase.
6) Where there is a **fundamental change in circumstances** which could not have been foreseen by the parties, for which neither party is responsible, and which would render performance of the contract fundamentally different from that which was reasonably contemplated by the parties. In **Metropolitan Water Board -v- Dick, Kerr and Co Ltd** (1918) it was held that the government's interference, under statutory powers with the construction of a reservoir was sufficient to frustrate the contract as once the contract was resumed, it would be radically different from the contract before interruption.

5.26 **Effects of Frustration**

The contract is automatically discharged, i.e. rendered void. This means, of course, that the party who was unable to perform his obligations is not liable for breach of contract and therefore there is no question of his having to pay damages.

The old common law rule was that the loss lay where it fell. This worked harshly in practice and therefore the **Law Reform (Frustrated Contracts) Act 1943** was passed and today regulates the position.

The Act provides as follows:-

1) In general, all money paid is repayable, all money payable ceases to be payable.
2) Where one party has incurred expense in performing or preparing to perform the contract (e.g. in manufacturing goods), then the court has a discretion to allow the party to retain payment, or recover payment, limited to the amount of the expense, from the other party.
3) Where one party has received a benefit under the contract (except the payment of money) e.g. an instalment of goods, he may be ordered to pay a sum equal to the benefit to the other party. Again the order is at the court's discretion.

The Act does not apply where the parties have inserted a clause into their contract dealing with the contingency which has arisen. The position would then be governed by the clause, not by the relating to frustration. However, the parties should take account of the **Unfair Contract Terms Act 1977.**

Certain types of contract are not governed by the 1943 Act e.g. contracts of insurance and those governed by the **Sale of Goods Act 1979.**

5.27 **Discharge by Agreement**

The parties may by mutual agreement **vary** the terms of a contract. It is common in building contracts for modifications to be made during the course of the work, i.e. the building will be different, usually at the request of the client, from the specification which formed part of the contract. As something different is done in substitution for the requirements of the original contract, this form of discharge of the original contract is described as **accord** and **satisfaction.** It should be noted that there can be oral variation of a written contract. However, where the contract is one which has to be evidenced in writing in order to be enforceable, any variation must also be evidenced in writing. However, it can be rescinded or cancelled by agreement without written evidence.

One party to a contract may request a complete **release** from his obligation under the contract. For example, Mr. Riddle telephones the hotel in which he has booked a room and cancels the booking. If the hotel refuses and Mr. Riddle insists, there is, of course, a breach of contract. However, it might suit the hotel to agree to the cancellation. If it does so, there is a binding release of both parties from the contract. The reason for this is that the release was supported by consideration on both sides: Mr. Riddle was released from his obligation to pay and the hotel was released from its obligation to provide the room. There is thus a mutual release from obligation and mutual surrender of benefit. This can only happen with an executory contract, i.e. one under which each party has yet to perform his obligations. Once one party has performed his obligations, there will be no consideration for his release of the other. This release will only be binding if made **under seal,** as no consideration is required for a deed. Where a creditor agrees to accept a smaller sum from the debtor in full satisfaction of the debt, he can generally sue for the balance because the debtor has given no consideration for the release of part of the debt. There are, however, exceptions to this rule, e.g. where a smaller amount was accepted before payment was due under the contract, i.e. the creditor gets the benefit of early payment; or where someone other than the debtor made the smaller payment by agreement with the creditor.

A party may grant some form of indulgence under an executory contract, e.g. he may agree to waive his strict right to insist on delivery of goods or performance of a service on the date fixed by the contract. If the other party relies upon this indulgence, the party granting it may be estopped from reverting, at least without notice or other good cause, to his strict rights even though no consideration was given for the forbearance or indulgence.

5.28 **Discharge by Acceptance of Breach**

Breach of a contract can occur in the following ways:-

1) One party may repudiate (i.e. refuse to be bound by) the contract before the date on which performance is required by the contract. This is known as **anticipatory breach.** The repudiation can be express, i.e. by the party

in breach stating, e.g. that he is not going to deliver the goods or render the service; or it can be implied from the fact that he disables himself from fulfilling his obligations, e.g. he sells the intended subject matter of the contract to someone else or emigrates so that he cannot render the service. The repudiation enables the innocent party to sue immediately, i.e. he need not await the date fixed for performance to see whether the other party is going to change his mind and honour his commitments.

In **Hochster -v- De la Tour** (1853) Hochster was engaged by De la Tour in April as a courier for a European Tour which was to start on 1st June. Before this date, in fact on 11 May, De la Tour cancelled the arrangement. Hochster sued immediately for breach of contract and it was held that he was entitled to succeed.

If the innocent party does not accept the repudiation and therefore does not commence an action, he runs the risk of events relieving the other party of liability, e.g. by frustration of the contract through the outbreak of war as in **Avery -v- Bowden** (1856), if he, the innocent party, becomes unable to fulfill his own obligations, he will not be able to recover damages.

2) One party may repudiate the contract by refusing to continue performing his obligations. Again the **repudiation** may be either express or implied. If a builder announces that he is not going to do any more work when half-way through erecting a house, that is express repudiation. If he simply leaves the site and does not return, that is implied repudiation or abandonment.

3) One party may render a defective performance of the contract. He may break either a **condition** of the contract or a **warranty.**

A **condition** is a **major term** of a contract, i.e. one that goes to the root of the contract. Breach of condition entitles the innocent party to treat the contract as repudiated and discharged, i.e. to refuse to perform his own obligations, e.g. to pay. In addition he can claim damages, however, he can, if he prefers, treat the breach of condition as a **breach of warranty** and **merely sue for damages.** Thus if there is a breach of a condition implied by the **Sale of Goods Act 1979,** e.g. the goods do not correspond with the sample, the buyer can reject the goods and refuse to pay, or he can accept the goods and treat the breach as a breach of warranty only. The buyer should, however, make clear that he is doing this, otherwise he may be taken to have waived the breach altogether.

5.29 Rights of the innocent party

Where there is a repudiation or breach of condition by the other party, the innocent party may treat the contract as discharged and thus regard himself as released from his own obligations; he may also claim damages. Alternatively he may affirm, i.e. continue with the contract and claim damages.

5.30 **Remedies for Breach of Contract**

The common law remedy is **damages** and an award is made of right if the innocent party can prove his case.

The **measure** (i.e. amount) of damages is the financial loss suffered by the innocent party. He is entitled to be placed, financially, in the same position as if the contract has been duly performed. If he has suffered no loss, he is entitled to nominal damages only. e.g. £2. Moreover, he is likely to find that he has to bear the other side's costs. Thus if a hotelier double books a room, so that, when Mr. and Mrs. Duncan who booked it arrive, there is no room for them, the hotelier will have to pay the difference between the price of the room and other accommodation which the disappointed guests are obliged to take, i.e. in another similar hotel. The hotelier will also have to pay the cost of travelling to the second hotel, similarly, where a seller fails to deliver goods to a buyer and the buyer has to pay more than the contract price for similar goods elsewhere, the seller will have to pay the extra by way of damages.

Not all damage resulting from a breach of contract is recoverable. The leading case with regard to remoteness of damage is **Hadley -v- Baxendale** (1854) in which a Gloucester miller entrusted a broken crankshaft to a carrier for transportation to an engineer for copying. The carrier was guilty of delay and the mill stood idle, i.e. resulting in a total loss of profits for the miller. It was held by the House of Lords that the claim failed as the carrier had not been informed that he was carrying the only crankshaft. Two rules emerged from this case:-

1) The party in breach is liable for such damage as arises **naturally, in the ordinary course of events,** from the breach; and
2) he is liable for damage which may reasonably be considered to have been in the **contemplation of the parties** at the time that they made the contract, i.e. he is liable for some special factor of which he knew or, the court decides, must have known.

The operation of these rules is clearly shown in the case of **Victoria Laundry (Windsor) Ltd -v- Newman Industries Ltd** (1949) in which Newman agreed to install a boiler for the laundry, but there was a delay of some five months. The laundry claimed (i) loss of profits on their ordinary laundry business and (ii) loss of profits on some exceptionally profitable dyeing contracts with the Ministry of Supply. It was held that claim (i) succeeded under the first rule stated above, but claim (ii) failed because Newman could not have contemplated the exceptional loss.

If unusual damage may result from a breach of contract, it is important that the other party is made aware of this fact before the contract is made so that he contracts on the basis of this knowledge and accepts responsibility for the possible loss. Thus if Newman had known of item (ii), there would have been liability for this head of loss.

5.31 **Duty of Mitigation**

The victim of a breach of contract must take reasonable steps to mitigate his loss, i.e. to keep his loss to a minimum. For example, B orders coal from S in July at £100 per ton, the agreed delivery being 1st September. S fails to make delivery on the agreed date.

The price of coal rises to £110 per ton on 1st October and to £120 ton on 1st November.

B delays getting an alternative supply until 1st November.

If B could have obtained supplies on 1st October, he will be able to recover only the difference between the contract price of £100 and £110, i.e. £10 per ton. He will not recover the full difference of £20 which he in fact pays.

If a supplier of goods is the victim of a breach of a contract, he should try to place the wrongfully rejected goods elsewhere, e.g. sell them. However, if he can meet all demands for his goods from existing stocks, he is not under a duty to sell the rejected goods — **Interoffice Telephones Ltd -v- Robert Freeman and Co Ltd** (1957).

5.32 **Liquidated Damages and Penalties**

Sometimes the parties agree, at the time of making the contract, the amount of damages payable in the event of breach. The damages are then described as **Liquidated,** i.e. ascertained or quantified as opposed to unliquidated, i.e. to be assessed by the court. The courts will enforce a liquidated damages clause provided that it is a genuine estimate of the possible loss. If the amount inserted in the contract exceeds the greatest loss which could result from breach, it will be struck out by the court as a penalty, i.e. it will be void; the court will then make its own assessment of damages.

If the parties find in retrospect that they have agreed too small a sum in relation to the actual loss, only the agreed (i.e. the liquidated) sum is payable **Cellulose Acetate Silk Co -v- Widness Foundry** (1933).

5.33 **Quantum Meruit**

This form of claim is an appropriate alternative to a claim for damages in certain circumstances, e.g. where work has been done under a void contract or where a contract is cancelled by one party, i.e. repudiated, after the innocent party has done preparatory work. The innocent party is then paid according to the value of work done, as in **Planche -v- Colburn** (1831) in which Planche agreed with Colburn to write for Colburn's periodical called The Juvenile Library. When Planche had written part of the work, Colburn discontinued the periodical. It was held that Planche was entitled to recover on quantum meruit (i.e. as much work as he had earned).

However, in the case of a lump-sum contract, e.g. a contract to erect a building at a fixed price without any mention of stage payments, there is an implied condition that the contract shall be completely performed before payment is due as in **Sumpter -v- Hedges** (1898) in which a building was left half-finished and a claim for payment for work and materials failed.

A claim on a quantum meruit is a quasi-contractual claim, not a claim under the original contract.

5.34 **Equitable Remedies**

It will be recalled that these are **specific performance, injunction, rescission** and **rectification** and that they are all discretionary remedies.

Specific performance is only granted where damages would not be an adequate remedy, i.e. where the subject-matter of the contract is unique, e.g. an original painting, and, more commonly in sales of land. It is never granted to compel the performance of a personal service.

An **injunction** can be either prohibitory or mandatory. A prohibitory injunction restrains someone from doing something, e.g. from breaking a negative stipulation in a contract such as a clause in a contract of employment restraining the employee from setting up in rival business or working for a rival employer within X years of leaving the employment and within X radius of his employer's premises.

Rescission is granted in cases of misrepresentation and in some cases of mistake but only where the decree would not divest an innocent purchaser of his rights.

5.35 **Interpretation of Contracts**

It is presumed by the courts that a written agreement expresses the parties' intentions: they are therefore not at liberty to adduce oral (or parol) evidence to vary its terms. However, there are exceptions to this general rule, as follows:-

1) Where the contract is not of a type that must be in writing, oral evidence can be admitted to show that it does not contain all the agreed terms, e.g. to show that there was a collateral warranty.
2) Where there is a latent (i.e. not obvious) ambiguity in the contract, parol evidence may be admitted to clarify the meaning. However, if on one construction (i.e. interpretation) of an ambiguous term, one party would be favoured, and on the other construction the other party would be favoured, the term is construed (i.e. interpreted) **contra proferentem.** This means that the interpretation which favours the person who did not draw up the contract is the one to be preferred. Thus the term is construed against the interests of the one who inserted it into the contract.
3) Parol evidence may be admitted to prove that a trade usage should be incorporated into the contract, but not where the trade usage is expressly excluded.
4) Evidence may be admitted to show that a written contract has been rescinded by oral agreement.

5) Evidence may be admitted to prove that the contract was made subject to a condition precedent, i.e. a condition which was to be fulfilled before the contract would come into operation, e.g. that the approval of some person was to be obtained and was not in fact obtained, as in **Pym -v- Campbell** (1856).

The judges give to words and phrases their ordinary meaning and to technical words the meaning given to them in the business context in which they are used, e.g. the phrase 'subject to average' in insurance business. Other rules for the interpretation of meaning are the same as for the interpretation of statutes, e.g. that the document must be construed as a whole. It should be noted that where a typewritten or printed document has been altered, e.g. by handwriting, the handwriting prevails in the event of inconsistency. Therefore an endorsement to a printed policy of insurance would prevail over the printed wording.

5.36 **Limitation of Actions**

If a plaintiff has a right of action for breach of contract, he must commence that action by the issue of a summons or a writ within the relevant period laid down by the **Limitation Act 1980.** If the plaintiff fails to do so, his right of action becomes statute-barred: this means that the defendant can plead the defence of limitation and the plaintiff's action will be struck out. The periods of limitation run from the accrual of the cause of action, i.e. the breach of contract, e.g. the failure to repay a loan on the date specified or the failure to deliver goods on a certain date.

The main periods of limitation are as follows:-

1) for breach of a simple contract, **six years** from the accrual of the cause of action;
2) for breach of a contract under seal, **twelve years** from the accrual of the cause of action;
3) for actions involving personal injuries, **three years,** generally, from the accrual of the cause of action or 'date of knowledge', if later.

Where the plaintiff was under a legal disability, i.e. was a minor or insane at the time of accrual of the right of action, time does not run until the infant became an adult or the insane person regained his sanity or from the time of the person's death if this occurred first. However, in actions involving personal injuries to a minor, time does run against him immediately unless he was not in the custody of a parent or guardian. Once time has begun to run, subsequent insanity does not stop it from running.

In relation to actions for non-payment of money, it should be noted that a statute-barred debt can be revived by the debtor acknowledging the debt to his creditor in writing and duly signing the acknowledgement. An acknowledgement will, of course, start time running afresh, even if the debt is not statute-barred. A part payment has a similar effect.

Where the action is based upon the fraud of the dependant, or the right of action is concealed by the defendant or the action is for relief from the consequences of mistake, time does not run until the fraud or mistake is discovered, or could, with reasonable diligence, have been discovered by the plaintiff. Thus if builders cover up foundations which they know to be inadequate and which will result in the subsidence of the building, there will be a fraudulent concealment of the right of action and if the builders raise the defence of limitation, it will fail, as in **King -v- Victor Parsons and Co** (1973). In some circumstances the court has power to extend time limits, e.g. under S.33 of the Act.

CHAPTER 6.

LAW OF AGENCY

6.01 GENERAL PRINCIPLES

The function of an agent is to **bring about a contract between** the person who instructed him, called **the principal**, and **a third party**, i.e. simply, someone else. Thus if the managing director of a manufacturing company contracts on behalf of the company to sell some of its products to a lawyer, the company is the principal, the managing director is the agent and the buyer is the third party. Once the contract has been made, the general rule is that rights and liabilities thereby created are between the principal and the third party and the agent simply 'drops out of the picture' i.e. he can neither sue the third party nor be sued by him.

The law looks, of course, at the reality of the relationship, not simply at the labels used, thus the fact that someone describes himself as an agent, does not necessarily mean that he is one. A garage may advertise that it is an agent for a certain car manufacturer. It will almost certainly be trading in the cars on its own account, i.e. will not be selling on behalf of the manufacturer and no contract will arise between the customer and the manufacturer. Therefore, the garage is not an agent in the legal sense.

Employees are sometimes agents of their employer, e.g. a shop assistant contracts with the customer on behalf of the shop. Many employees are not agents, e.g. cleaners and production workers.

Anyone with contractual capacity can appoint an agent, conversely, a person without capacity, e.g. an insane person, cannot appoint and if he does so no authority will be conferred.

6.02 CREATION OF AGENCY

Agency may be created by express agreement between principal and agent, i.e. the agent accepts instructions from the principal; by contract; by necessity and by ratification.

Express Agreement

The appointment of the agent may be made verbally or in writing. However, where the agent is required to enter into a deed, the appointment must be made under seal. i.e. by Power of Attorney in accordance with the **Powers of Attorney Act 1971**.

By Conduct

If one person holds out (i.e. represents another person as his agent), whether by words or conduct, he will be bound by a transaction into which that other enters. For example, P has engaged A an impecunious builder to build him a house. A obtains the materials that he requires and directs the supplier to send the accounts to P. If P settles the accounts it will be reasonably assumed by the supplier that A is P's agent. Therefore if P refuses to pay an account, the supplier can sue him. In other words, P is estopped by his conduct of settling the accounts from denying that A had authority to place orders for materials on his behalf.

By Necessity

An agency of necessity arises where A is entrusted with the property of P and A finds it necessary to take steps to preserve it, e.g. a horse is sent by rail and when it reaches its destination, there is no one there to receive it. Clearly, the railway authority cannot abandon the horse; it has authority by virtue of agency of necessity to make a contract on behalf of the owner to have the horse put in a stable and fed for the night, as in **Great Northern Railway -v- Swaffield** (1874). It is less likely that this type of agency will arise these days as modern communications enable the bailee (the person to whom the goods are entrusted) to take the owner's instructions.

By Ratification

Ratification is the adoption by a principal of a contract which was made without authority or in excess of authority by the agent. The ratification is, in effect, an authority given after the event. To authorise an act is to give permission before the act; to ratify an act is to endorse it or take it over after it has occurred.

Certain conditions have to be fulfilled for ratification to be valid, i.e. to bind the principal to the contract as effectively as if he had authorised it:-

1. The agent must contract as agent and this fact must be known to the other party. If the agent intends to contract as agent without informing the other party of his intention, there can be no ratification.
2. The principal should either be named or ascertainable when the contract is made.
3. The principal must have been in existence when the contract was made and have contractual capacity, e.g. a company formed only after the making of the contract cannot ratify it.
4. The principal must have full knowledge of the material facts at the time of ratification or he must have decided to ratify the contract whatever the true facts may be.

Ratification **relates back** to the date of the original contract so that the principal becomes entitled to all the benefits and subject to all the liabilities. Nevertheless, ratification cannot operate so as to divest an innocent third party of rights acquired in the subject matter between the making of the contract and the act of ratification, e.g. the rights of a trustee in bankruptcy.

A contract which the agent makes 'subject to ratification' does not become binding unless and until ratified.

6.03 AUTHORITY OF THE AGENT

The authority of the agent may be **actual**, **usual**, **implied** or **apparent**.

If Auntie Beverley gives Niece Teresa instructions to buy her some winter woollies from the Homely Department Store and Teresa does so, Teresa has actual or real authority to do so.

If Auntie Beverley has been in the habit of sending Niece Teresa to make purchases for her and get her account debited at the Homely Department Store, Niece Teresa will have acquired usual or apparent authority in the eyes of the store. The store will have rendered accounts to Auntie Beverley following the purchases and will have received her cheques in settlement. If one day Niece Teresa buys a 'see through' nightdress, Auntie Beverley will have to pay for it even though Niece Teresa had no authority to make so frivolous a purchase.

Thus **usual** or **apparent** authority can arise through **a course of dealings**. It can also arise because of the **profession of the agent**, e.g. that of insurance broker, architect, solicitor, accountant, managing director of a company. There may of course, be limits on the authority of such people, but other people will not know of these limits. Thus the other contracting party places reliance upon the normal authority of the professional person and he is entitled to do so, i.e. the principal will be bound by the resultant contract.

In **Panorama Developments Ltd -v- Fidelis Furnishing Fabrics Ltd** (1971) the company Secretary of Fidelis hired expensive cars from Panorama in the name of Fidelis. He had no actual authority to do so and in fact used the cars for his own private purposes. It was held that Fidelis was liable for the hire charges as a company secretary has usual or apparent authority to make this type of contract on behalf of the company.

The other contracting party will obtain a valid contract with the principal where usual or apparent authority exists, even if the principal has expressly forbidden the agent to enter into the contract in question. In **Watteau -v- Fenwick** (1893) the manager of a public house was forbidden by the owner to purchase cigars. However, he did so. It was held that the owner of the pub was liable to the suppliers.

A **partner** has usual or implied authority under *S.5* of the **Partnership Act 1890** to make contracts which are within the scope of the firm's business, e.g. to purchase goods usually used in that business. Therefore if, at a meeting, the partners resolve that no partner shall place an order for goods in excess of £5,000 without the consent of the other, and one of the partners places an order for £6,000 worth of usual goods without such consent, the other partners will be bound by the contract.

If the other contracting party is aware of the agent's lack of authority or of the limitation upon that authority then, of course, the principal would not be bound. The law is designed to protect innocent outsiders and, clearly, an outsider who is, or should be, aware of the true facts needs no protection. It should be noted that the terms **'usual'**, **'implied'** or **'apparent'** authority overlap: usual authority will always be apparent and any form of authority which is not express must be implied, i.e. arise by necessary implication from the facts. Apparent authority is also commonly referred to as 'ostensible' authority.

6.04 THE RIGHTS AND LIABILITIES CREATED BY A CONTRACT MADE BY AN AGENT

The rights and liabilities of the principal, agent and other contracting party depend upon the circumstances in which the contract was made. Three separate situations need to be considered:-

1. **Where the agent contracts on behalf of a named principal**
   The general rule is that the agent can neither sue the other contracting party nor be sued by him, but there are exceptions to this rule, e.g. where the custom of the trade makes the agent liable or the agent executes a deed in his own name.
2. **Where the agent contracts on behalf of an unnamed principal**
   This means that the agent discloses to the other contracting party the existence of a principal, but does not identify or name that principal. As the other party is aware that he is dealing with an agent, the agent is not personally liable. If the agent fails to make it clear that he is acting merely as an agent then, of course, he will incur personal liability.
3. **Where the agent contracts on behalf of an undisclosed principal**
   In this case, the other contracting party believes that the agent is the principal; moreover he has no means of knowing the reality of the situation. Therefore, he, the other party, can sue the agent as if he were the principal. Once the principal emerges, the position is as follows:
   (a) the principal can sue the other contracting party;
   (b) the other party can elect (i.e. choose) to sue either the principal or the agent.

If the other party exercises his election against either principal or agent, he cannot sue the other one at a later date, e.g. if he fails to obtain satisfaction from the judgment.

There are, however, the following exceptions to the rule that the principal can sue and the other party can elect whom to sue:

(a) Where the rule would operate contrary to the express or implied terms of the contract, e.g. **where the personality of the agent is important** as in a contract of employment; or

(b) where the agent had **no actual authority** from the principal or had exceeded his authority.

It will be readily appreciated that actual or real authority is a condition of the application of the doctrine of the undisclosed principal: there can of course, be no question of any other type of authority in view of the fact that the other contracting party is ignorant of the existence of the principal at the time of making the contract.

Where there is a valid intervention by the principal so that he takes the benefit and becomes subject to the burden of the contract, he can be faced with any defence which the other contracting party could have raised against the agent, e.g. a right of set-off as in **Montague -v- Forwood** (1873).

Whether the principal is named, unnamed or initially undisclosed, he is liable for the fraud or other tort, e.g. negligence, of his agent whilst the latter was acting as agent, as in **Lloyd -v- Grace, Smith & Co.** (1912) in which a managing clerk in a firm of solicitors fraudulently induced a client to convey properties to him. It was held that the firm was liable for the fraud.

6.05 BREACH OF WARRANTY OF AUTHORITY

As we have seen, the agent may have actual authority, e.g. to sign a receipt for a debt due to his principal, or he may have apparent authority to do so, e.g. from the custom of a trade. However, the agent may, in fact, enter into a contract without any form of authority whatsoever. In this case, the principal will not be bound and the other contracting party may sue the agent for breach of warranty of authority, i.e. for representing that he had authority when in fact he had none. The agent will be liable whether he acted innocently or fraudulently and even though his authority has been automatically revoked, without his knowledge, by the death or insanity of his principal. The measure of damages will be the loss suffered by the other contracting party.

6.06 RIGHTS AND DUTIES EXISTING BETWEEN PRINCIPAL AND AGENT

The duties of an agent are as follows:

1. **To act in accordance with his principal's instructions.** He must not exceed his authority: it is no excuse that he did so in what he believed to be the principal's best interests. He will not be liable to the principal where he interprets ambiguous instructions reasonably; but he should, of course, always seek clarification where this is possible.

   If an agent binds his principal to a contract which is within his apparent authority, but not within his real or actual authority, the principal can sue him for the loss which the principal sustains.
2. **To perform his duties personally**, i.e. **not to delegate** performance to someone else. However, delegation may be permitted by the express terms of the agent's appointment or by custom. If delegation is permissible then the agent will be responsible for the acts of his delegates.
3. **To take reasonable care** in the performance of his duties and to use any special skill which is implied by his membership of a profession, e.g. the skill expected of an insurance broker, solicitor etc. This applies even if the agency is gratuitous.

4. **Not to allow a conflict of interest** to arise between himself and his principal. He must safeguard his principal's interests and not seek personal advantage, apart, naturally, from normal remuneration. The relationship is a fiduciary one, i.e. based upon trust. This means that the agent must make a full disclosure of material facts to his principal, e.g. if he wishes to buy his principal's property or if he wishes to compete in any way with the principal. If the agent accepts a bribe or secret commission he is liable to prosecution under the **Prevention of Corruption Acts 1889-1916**. The principal can recover the bribe and sue both the agent and the giver of the bribe for the loss suffered.
   In addition the agent must not make use of any confidential information disclosed to him during the course of his agency. Any breach of the duty of good faith entitles the principal:
   (a) to refuse to pay the agent's remuneration and expenses;
   (b) to dismiss the agent;
   (c) to sue to recover damages for any loss suffered.
5. **To account to the principal** for money received on behalf of the principal.

It should be noted that the duties of an agent are the same as the common law duties owed by an employee to his employer.

The duties of a principal are as follows:

1. **To pay the agent the agreed remuneration**, e.g. commission. If no express agreement is made as to the amount of remuneration, it will be decided according to the customs of the trade or profession in question or will be such sum which, in the opinion of the court, is reasonable.
2. **To indemnify** the agent for all expenses properly incurred in the performance of his duties.

It should be noted that an agent has a **lien** over his principal's goods until payment has been made or tendered by the principal. A lien is a right to retain a debtor's goods pending settlement of the debt. The right is lost once the agent has parted with the goods, except where he was induced to part with possession through fraud.

6.07 TERMINATION OF AGENCY

The agency can be terminated **by the parties themselves** or **by operation of law**.

The parties may agree to bring the agency to an end; the **principal may revoke** the agent's authority or the **agent may renounce** the agency. The contract of agency may be discharged by performance, by or effluxion of time where it was entered into for a fixed period and that period has expired. It may also be discharged by frustration, e.g. where the principal or agent acquire the status of an enemy through the outbreak of war.

The termination may amount to a breach of contract in which case damages will be payable by the party in breach.

It is most important to note that a revocation of an agent's authority will not affect other contracting parties until they are informed of it, i.e. the revocation will then prevent the formation of contracts in the future, but will not affect any contract already made.

If the principal gave the agent authority coupled with an interest, e.g. as a means of recouping debts due from the principal to the agent, the agency is irrevocable until there is no more indebtedness remaining.

Agency is terminated by operation of law (i.e. automatically, independently of the wishes of the parties) by **death, bankruptcy** and **insanity**. Death is a matter of public record, i.e. a death certificate is issued, and as a result the personal representatives of the deceased will not be liable on a contract made by the deceased's agent after the date of death. On bankruptcy, the rights of the bankrupt, with some exceptions, pass to the trustee in bankruptcy who has a right to disclaim onerous contracts. Insanity is a private event and therefore the insane principal will be bound by a contract made before the insanity became known to the other contracting party, as in **Drew -v- Nunn** (1879). However, the agent will be liable to the insane principal because he has acted without actual authority.

The position may be different if the appointment of the agent is by deed under the Enduring Powers of Attorney Act 1985. Provided that the appropriate formalities have been complied with the subsequent insanity or incapability of the principal will **not** affect the agent's authority.

DELEGATION BY AGENTS

As note above the general rule is that the agent must not delegate his duties but delegation is allowed in the following cases:-

1. Where the principal is aware **at the time of the creation of the agency relationship** that the agent intends to delegate his authority **and** the principal in no way objects to this.
2. Where from the circumstances of the case and the conduct of the parties it can be presumed that the agent was intended to have power to delegate his authority.
3. Where delegation of authority or the employment of a sub agent is a usual practice in the trade in which the agent is engaged and it is not unreasonable or inconsistent with the express terms of the agency agreement.
4. Wherever the agent's authority is such as to require, wholly or in part, with the assistance of another person or persons.
5. Where such delegation becomes necessary because of unforeseen circumstances.

CHAPTER 7.

TORTS

7.01 **TORTIOUS LIABILITY**

Liability in tort is normally founded on **fault** but there are exceptions, i.e. cases of **strict liability**.

7.02 **NEGLIGENCE**

The most important tort in modern times is **negligence**. The plaintiff must prove the following essentials in order to succeed in his action:

1. That the defendant owed him a **duty of care**;
2. That the duty was **broken**; and
3. That the plaintiff **suffered damage** as a result.

Thus negligence is more than merely carelessness. Carelessness is, however, one elemtnt of the tort.

The duty of care

Whether a duty exists in any particular case is a question of law. The leading case on this point is **Donoghue -v- Stevenson** (1921) in which a man took a lady friend for refreshment in a cafe in Paisley, Scotland, and bought her a bottle of ginger beer. She drank some of the contents and then poured the remainder into her glass. At this point there floated out, from the depths of the opaque bottle, the decomposing remains of a snail! The lady was very ill as a result. The lady could not sue the seller, i.e. the cafe proprietor, as she was not a party to the contract of sale. She therefore sued the manufacturer in the tort of negligence.

The question which the House of Lords had to decide was whether any duty was owed to her by the manufacturer. It was held that a manufacturer does owe a duty of care to the ultimate consumer of his product where there is no opportunity for examination of the product before use.

Lord Atkin stated that there is a general principle underlying all the cases on the tort of negligence, the principle being that we owe a duty of care to our neighbour. He said: "You must take reasonable care to avoid acts or omissions which you can reasonably foresee would be likely to injure your neighbour." He then said: "Who then is my neighbour? The answer seems to be persons who are so closely and directly affected by my act that I ought reasonably to have them in contemplation as being so affected when I am directing my mind to the acts or omissions which are called in question."

Thus **reasonable foreseeability of injury** or damage to one's neighbour is a pre-requisite of liability in negligence. Moreover, each defendant is judged according to what a reasonable defendant, i.e. a reasonable defendant would have foreseen, not according to what the particular defendant, who may be a most unreasonable man, foresaw.

The application of this principle can be seen in the following cases:-

Home Office -v- Dorset Yacht Co. (1970)

Some borstal boys were on a training exercise on Brownsea Island in Portland Harbour. One night, whilst their officers, in defiance of instructions, were all in bed, the boys escaped and caused severe damage to the plaintiff's yacht. It was argued on behalf of the Home Office that no duty was owed to any member of the public (in other words, the duty imposed by the relevant statute was owed to the Crown alone). This argument was rejected and it was held that the plaintiff was indeed a 'neighbour' in relation to the Home Office, i.e. that a duty of care was owed to the plaintiff.

Anns -v- Merton London Borough Council (1978)

The plaintiffs were owners of flats in a block built in 1962. In 1970 cracks appeared in the structure of the building which indicated subsidence. The plaintiffs sued both the builder and the local authority alleging that the subsidence was due to the inadequacy of the foundations. They alleged that the Council was negligent either in failing to inspect the foundations or in failing, through their building inspector, to notice the inadequacy when they did inspect. It was argued that the Council could not be liable as they were merely empowered by the **Public Health Act 1936** to make inspections to check compliance with the bye-laws, i.e. they had no duty to make inspections. It was held, however, that the Council were under a duty to 'make their discretionary decisions responsibly and for reasons that accord with the statutory purpose' and did therefore owe a duty of care to the plaintiffs.

Bourhill -v- Young (1943)

The plaintiff, Mrs. Bourhill, who was a fishwife and eight months pregnant, heard, but could not see, a collision between the motor-cycle of the deceased Mr. Young and a car. The accident which occurred in an Edinburgh street was due to the deceased's negligence. The plaintiff was sueing the deceased's estate alleging that the deceased owed her a duty of care and that she had suffered severe nervous shock through his breach of that duty. It was held that no duty was owed to her as it was not reasonably foreseeable that such injury would be suffered by her. She was not therefore a 'neighbour' of the deceased. The test of liability for nervous shock is therefore foreseeability of causing injury by nervous shock.

McLoughlin -v- O'Brian (1982)

A mother, who was at home, was informed by a witness that her family had been involved in a serious road accident some two miles away. She rushed to the hospital where she saw two of her children severely injured, her husband in a state of nervous shock and learnt that the third child had died. She suffered severe shock, organic depression and a change of personality as a result of this experience. It was held that the defendant did owe a duty of care to the mother as she came upon the 'immediate aftermath' of the accident. Thus, although the accident occurred out of her sight and hearing, her illness was a reasonably foreseeable consequence.

There can be liability for **negligent words** as well as for neighbour acts in certain circumstances. The leading case is **Hedley Byrne and Co. -v- Heller and Partners Ltd** (1964) in which a bank gave a reference concerning the credit worthiness of a customer company to an enquirer, but subject to a disclaimer of all liability. The bank stated that their customer was a "... respectably constituted company, considered good for its ordinary business engagements." The plaintiff (i.e. the enquirer) then suffered substantial loss when the company went into liquidation. It was held that the bank was protected by its disclaimer of liability. However, it was made clear that there would have been liability if there had been no disclaimer. Thus liability for a negligent statement will arise where the person making the statement realises or should realise that the recipient of the statement is likely to rely upon it. **No contract between maker and recipient is necessary**, but a 'special relationship' is necessary. Such a 'special relationship' was created in the case of **Nettleship -v- Weston** (1971) in which a learner driver and her husband assured a friend that he would be covered by insurance if he were to give the learner driver driving lessons. It was held that this assurance was an assumption of responsibility towards the friend on which the friend was entitled to rely. This case is thus the converse of Hedley Byrne in that the assurance created a liability that would not otherwise have existed.

Hedley Byrne also established that purely economic or financial loss which resulted from negligent words could be recovered. In **Sparton Steel and Alloys Ltd -v- Martin and Co. (Contractors) Ltd** (1973) it was held that economic loss which is independent of physical damage is irrecoverable. However, recovery for purely economic loss was allowed in the House of Lords' case of **Junior Books Ltd -v- The Veitchi Co. Ltd** (1982) in which the defective work of a flooring subcontractor caused loss to the factory owner. However, it was stressed in this case that there was a special relationship between the owner and the subcontractor which fell only just short of a contractual relationship. It would therefore be wrong to suppose that in all cases purely economical loss is recoverable.

7.03 BREACH OF THE DUTY

It is not sufficient that the plaintiff proves that the defendant owed him a duty of care. He must also prove that there was a breach of that duty, i.e. that the defendant failed to take reasonable care. Whether there was such a failure is a question of fact, not law. The fact that the damage which occurred was reasonably foreseeable will not in itself render the defendant liable. The context in which the damage occurred must be considered, i.e. the objective which the defendant was trying to achieve, the nature of the risk, its likelihood and magnitude. Lord Justice Asquith said in **Daborn -v- Bath Tramways** (1946): "The purpose behind the defendant's conduct, if sufficiently important justifies the assumption of abnormal risk."

Lord Denning said in **Watt -v- Hertfordshire County Council** (1954): "It is well settled that in measuring due care you must balance the risk against the measures necessary to eliminate the risk. To that proposition there ought to be added this: you must balance the risk against the end to be achieved."

In the latter case, an injured fireman did not succeed in a claim in negligence against his employers because the nature of the emergency (a woman trapped under a bus some short distance away) justified the fireman being sent to the scene in a vehicle in which a heavy jack (for lifting heavy weights) could not be properly secured and which just caught the plaintiff fireman's ankle when the driver had to brake suddenly. If there had been no emergency, the injured employee would undoubtedly have succeeded against his employers.

A duty of reasonable care is also owed to persons who suffer from a disability, e.g. the blind in circumstances where their presence is reasonably to be expected, e.g. in city streets as was decided in **Haley -v- London Electrity Board** (1964) in which a blind man was injured by an obstruction left on the highway. The defendants were liable as his presence was foreseeable and the obstruction was a real danger to the blind.

Where the plaintiff alleges negligence in a professional person, i.e. a person professing to have a special skill, he must prove that the defendant did not exercise the standard of skill and care which is shown by 'the ordinary skilled man exercising and professing to have that special skill' — per McNair J. in **Bolam -v- Friern Hospital Management Committee** (1957).

7.04 THE BURDEN OF PROOF

It is for the plaintiff to prove on a balance of probabilities that the defendant has broken his duty of care. However, there are some situations in which it can readily be stated that there must have been negligence on the part of the defendant; in other words the accident could not have occurred without negligence on his part. The maxim applied is **res ipsa loquitur** ('The facts speak for themselves'). The effect of the maxim is to reverse the burden of proof, i.e. it is then necessary for the defendant to disprove negligence. In **Mahon -v- Osborne** (1939) a swab was found in a patient's body following an operation. It was held that the maxim applied. In **Walsh -v- Holst and Co. Ltd.** (1958) a brick fell from a building under the control of the defendants and injured the plaintiff. However, the defendants were able to prove that they had a safe system. It was held that the maxim had no further application and the defendants were not liable.

7.05 CAUSATION

Finally, the plaintiff must prove the third element of the tort of negligence, namely, that the damage resulted from the defendant's breach of duty. In **Barnett -v- Chelsea and Kensington Hospital Management Committee** (1968), a hospital doctor was guilty of a breach of duty in failing to examine a man who came to the casualty department complaining of vomiting. The man died later of arsenic poisoning. It was held that the defendants were not liable as the man would have died whether he had been examined or not. The defendant will not, of course, be liable for damage or injury suffered by the plaintiff which arises, not from the defendant's negligence, but from some entirely new cause, or **novus actus interveniens** e.g. the unreasonable behaviour of the plaintiff in exposing himself to hazards after injury, or the act of a third party.

Moreover, some damage may be too remote a consequence of the negligence. It was laid down in **Overseas Tankship (U.K.) Ltd. -v- Morts Dock and Engineereing Co** (1961), known as The Wagon Mound, by the Judicial Committee of the Privy Council that the defendant is only liable for such damage as is a reasonably foreseeable consequence of his negligent act.

7.06 CONTRIBUTORY NEGLIGENCE

Even where the plaintiff succeeds in proving the three essential elements of negligence, he may be met with a claim of contributory negligence by the defendant. Under the Law Reform (Contributory Negligence) Act 1945 damages awarded against a defendant are reduced by a proportion which reflects the contributory fault of the plaintiff, if any. In **Sayers -v- Harlow U.D.C.** (1958), Mrs. Sayers found herself locked into a Council lavatory. She attempted to escape by climbing over the door, but did not succeed and decided to retreat. In doing so she fell and injured herself (as the toilet roll on which she had placed one foot rotated under her weight). Her claim against the Council succeeded as they had been negligent in failing to maintain their locks, but her damagses were reduced by 25 per cent on account of her contributory fault.

In **Baker -v- Willoughby** (1969) a driver of a car and a pedestrian had a clear view along a road for at least 200 yards, but the pedestrian stepped into the path of the car and was injured. It was held by the Court of Appeal that the pedestrian's damages should be reduced by 50 per cent to reflect his contributory fault.

In **Owens -v- Brimmell** (1976), the damages of a passenger were reduced on account of his taking a lift in a car with a driver whom he knew to be drunk. It is clear from modern cases such as **Froom -v- Butcher** (1975) and **O'Connell -v- Jackson** (1971) that the plaintiff's failure to wear a seat belt when travelling in or on a vehicle will result in a reduction of damages where the failure was material to the injuries suffered. Therefore, if the wearing of a seat belt would have made no difference, the damages will not be reduced.

7.07 VOLENTI NON FIT INJURIA

('he who consents to run a risk cannot complain'). This is a general defence to an action in tort, but it is of particular relevance in actions in negligence where the plaintiff alledgedly exposes himself to a risk of injury. A rescuer clearly exposes himself to such a risk in attempting to rescue a person who is in danger through the fault of another. At first sight the rescue may appear to be in the act of a third party for which the defendant has no responsibility. The courts will not allow the defendant to escape liability, however, where the danger which he created invited an attempt at rescue.

In **Haynes -v- Harwood** (1935) a policeman was injured when he intervened to prevent bolting horses from injuring people on the highway. It was held that the defendants, whose negligence in leaving the horses unattended had caused the accident, were liable to him as he had acted under a legal duty to prevent injury to life and limb. However, if there had been no real danger to anyone, then the plaintiff rescuer would doubtless not have succeeded, as in **Cutler -v- United Dairies (London) Ltd** (1933) in which the plaintiff was injured when trying to stop a horse which had bolted into a meadow.

In **Chadwick -v- British Railways Board** (1967), the plaintiff suffered severe nervous shock as a result of helping the victims of the Lewisham train disaster which was caused by the Board's negligence. The plaintiff acted solely from a sense of moral duty, but it was held that he was entitled to succeed in his claim. The defence of volenti may be raised against persons who participate in a sport or who are spectators. There are risks of injury necessarily incidental to many sports and those who expose themselves voluntarily to such risks cannot afterwards complain. Thus, if a participant in a fast moving sport makes an error of judgment in 'the agony of the moment' and a spectator is injured, there will be no liability. However, there would be liability if the participant (or the organisers) of a sport showed a 'reckless disregard of the spectator's safety'. In this case the defence of volenti would not succeed as the spectator could not have consented to this type of risk, as was made clear in **Woolridge -v- Sumner** (1963).

An employer will rarely succeed in raising this defence against an employee who may well know of a risk created by his employer's negligence, but will seldom have genuinely consented to it.

7.08 BREACH OF STATUTORY DUTY

The breach of a duty imposed by a statute is often a **criminal offence**, e.g. a breach of the employer's duty to ensure so far as is reasonably practicable the health, safety and welfare of his employees whilst they are at work under the **Health and Safety at Work Act 1974**. Whether the breach also gives rise to civil liability depends upon the wording of the individual statute.

A breach of the **Factories Act 1961** gives rise to both criminal and civil liability on the part of an employer; a breach of the **Health and Safety at Work Act** gives rise only to criminal liability.

7.09 EMPLOYERS' LIABILITY

An employer has duties under various statutes, as indicated above, and also basic common law duties. He must at common law provide safe premises, safe equipment, a safe system of work and competent fellow employees. Usually the same set of facts gives rise to both a breach of statutory duty and to negligence in which case it is normal practice for the plaintiff to plead in the alternative or to plead both. Where the statute in question creates strict liability, it is easier for the plaintiff to succeed in a claim for breach of statutory duty than in negligence as he has merely to prove breach of the duty and resultant damage, i.e. he does not have to prove carelessness.

7.10 OCCUPIERS' LIABILITY

The **Occupiers' Liability Act 1957** imposes on an occupier a common duty of care to a visitor, i.e. to any person who is lawfully present on the premises. The **common duty of care** is defined in S.2 of the Act as 'a duty to take such care as in all the circumstances of the case is reasonable to see that the visitor will be reasonably safe in using the premises for the purpose for which he is invited or permitted by the occupier to be there'. Premises include land, buildings, and 'any fixed or moveable structure, including any vessel, vehicle or aircraft'.

The Act specifically states that the occupier must be prepared for children to be less careful than adults.

With regard to persons who enter premises in exercise of their calling, i.e. tradesmen and workmen, e.g. plumbers, electricians, the occupier will not be liable for injury which results from special risks which are incidental to the calling, i.e. the job, of such a person. Therefore, if the electrician electrocutes himself, the occupier will not be liable. However, the occupier will only be free from liability so long as he leaves the workman free to guard against special risks. If the occupier interferes, he could well render himself liable. Moreover, if the injury to the workman results from a risk which is not incidental to his calling, e.g. the electrician trips and falls on a hole in the staircarpet, the occupier will be liable, as he would be to any visitor.

Where a visitor suffers injury or damage as a result of defective work done by a contractor engaged by the occupier, the occupier will not be liable if he has acted reasonably in entrusting the work to the contractor, i.e. if he has chosen a reputable contractor, and if he has made such check as is possible to see that the work has been properly done.

In **O'Connor -v- Swan and Edgar and Carmichael Contractors** (1963), the plaintiff, who was working as a demonstrator in the store belonging to Swan and Edgar, was injured when a piece of plaster fell from the ceiling onto her head. She sued Swan and Edgar as occupiers, but her claim failed; she also sued the plasterers in negligence and this claim succeeded.

The occupier can protect himself by a warning notice provided that the warning is sufficient to enable the visitor to be reasonably safe in using the premises for the purpose for which he was invited or permitted to be there. Thus if there were two means of access to a property, one safe and one unsafe and a notice warning the visitor not to use the unsafe one, but to enter via the safe one a short distance away, the notice would enable the visitor to be reasonably safe and would therefore protect the occupier from liability.

S.2(i) **Unfair Contract Terms Act 1977** provides that any notice displayed in the course of a business will not protect an occupier where death or personal injury is caused by the occupier's negligence. Any attempt by the occupier to exclude or restrict liability for other types of damage, e.g. damage to property, is subject to the reasonableness test.

The Act creates only a civil right of action, i.e. a right for the plaintiff to sue for damages; it does not impose criminal liability. However, criminal liability can arise in certain circumstances, under the **Health and Safety at Work Act**.

OCCUPIERS' LIABILITY ACT 1984

The law relating to trespassers is now contained in the 1984 Act. It provides that an occupier only owes a duty to a trespasser (a) where the occupier is aware of a danger on his premises or has reasonable grounds for believing in the existence of a danger; and (b) where he knows or has reasonable grounds for believing that the trespasser is near to the danger; and (c) where the risk is one against which the occupier may reasonably be expected to offer some protection. Where these conditions are fulfilled and therefore the duty exists, the duty is to take such care as is reasonable in all the circumstances of the case to see that he, the trespasser, does not suffer injury on the premises by reason of the danger. The occupier may in an appropriate case discharge his duty by a warning or some appropriate deterrence. There is no liability for damage to property resulting from a breach of duty and no duty owed to a trespasser who willingly accepts the risk.

7.11 TRESPASS

There are three types of trespass; **trespass to the person**, **trespass to goods** and **trespass to land**. All types of trespass are **actionable per se**, i.e. without proof of damage.

Trespass to the person can take the form of battery, which is the unlawful application of force, however slight, to another person against their will: assault, which is putting a person in fear of battery, e.g. by brandishing a knife; false imprisonment, which is the total restraint of a person's freedom of movement, e.g. by locking him in a room with no means of escape. The **defences** which may be raised in this tort are as follows:-

1. **Self-defence:** the degree of force which is lawful will depend upon the circumstances; the force used in defence should be proportionate to that used in the attack. 'Self-defence' extends to the defence of family and, possibly of any other person.

   Defence of Property: reasonable force may be used in the defence of property and an occupier may use reasonable force in ejecting a trespasser.
2. **Volenti non fit injuria**, i.e. consent. It is the signing of the consent form by a patient before hospital treatment that prevents the treatment constituting a trespass.
3. **Inevitable Accident:** if the act was neither intentional nor negligent, there will be no liability, as in **Stanley -v- Powell** (1891) in which a member of a shooting party shot at a pheasant, but the shot ricocheted off a tree and struck the plaintiff. As this was an unforeseeable occurrence, i.e. there was no negligence, the defendant was not liable.
4. **Parental Authority** and that of someone acting in loco parentis, e.g. a schoolmaster. Reasonable chastisement may be used in the punishment of a child.
5. **Judicial authority**, e.g. cases of imprisonment of a convicted person.

Trespass to goods is an unlawful interference with goods in the possession of another person. The interference must be either intentional or negligent. It could take the form of damaging goods or simply moving them about.

Conversion is an unlawful denial of another person's title to, i.e. ownership of goods or a dealing which is inconsistent with his right to immediate possession of the goods. The taking and keeping of another's goods, the refusal to return them, the destruction of them, or the sale of them are all acts of conversion. This tort can be committed either dishonestly or innocently. When the tort-feasor acts dishonestly the conversion is also the crime of theft. Cases of innocent conversion occur where a mistake has been made, e.g. by an auctioneer in selling goods which were not given to him by the owner for sale. We have seen in relation to the Law of Contract that where the contract between A and B is void for material mistake of fact, and B sells the subject matter of the contract to C, the contract between B and C is also void and both B and C can be sued by A in conversion. B may be a rogue, but may be completely innocent, as in **Cundy -v- Lindsay** (1878).

The law relating to wrongful interference with goods is now contained in **The Torts (Interference with Goods) Act 1977**.

Trespass to land is an unlawful interference with the possession of land. It can be committed innocently, e.g. by the trespasser crossing an unmarked boundary without being aware of the fact, by his erecting a fence or a building on land which he mistakenly believes belongs to him. Other examples of trespass are throwing things, e.g. rubbish, onto a neighbour's land, walking or driving onto another's land, remaining on another's land after permission has been withdrawn. The owner of the land owns not only the surface of the land, but also the air space above and the land below the suface: therefore, it is a trespass to interfere with either, e.g. be erecting a sign which overhangs one's neighbour's land or by excavating beneath it and laying a pipe or cable. Under the **Civil Aviation Act 1949** there is no liability for the passage of aircraft over land at a reasonable height, but there is strict liability for any damage caused by the aircraft.

Trespass 'ab initio' occurs where someone enters land by authority of law, e.g. a policeman with a warrant, and then abuses his right of entry by some positive act, e.g. by assaulting the occupier or stealing property. The person who initially entered lawfully becomes a trespasser from the moment of the abuse of his right; he is then deemed to be a trespasser 'ab initio', i.e. from the moment of entry.

'Trespassers will be prosecuted' is a warning often displayed by landowners. However, trespass is a civil wrong, not a crime, save in special cases, e.g. trespass onto a railway line.

Defences

There are the following special defences to an action for trespass to land:-

1. that the entry was made in exercise of lawful authority, e.g. under a court order;
2. that the entry was made under licence from the occupier, i.e. with express or implied permission;
3. that the entry was made in an emergency, e.g. to stop the progress of fire.

Remedies

These are as follows:-

1. Ejection of the trespasser. The occupier should normally first order the trespasser to leave and give him reasonable time to do so. If the trespasser does not leave, the occupier may eject him by using reasonable force.
2. An action for recovery of land, with or without an action for mesne profits, i.e. an action for loss suffered during the period of wrongful possession by the trespasser.
3. Damages and/or injunction.

7.12 NUISANCE

There are two kinds of nuisance: **public nuisance** and **private nuisance**.

PUBLIC NUISANCE is some form of unlawful interference with the lives, health, safety, comfort or convenience of the public or a section of the public. Examples are obstructions of the highway, the emission of fumes or smells from a factory. Public nuisance is primarily a crime and a prosecution can be brought by the police or the Attorney-General and an injunction may be sought in order to ensure that the nuisance is discontinued. An action for damages may be brought by a person who suffers special damage, i.e. not merely inconvenience suffered in common with others. Thus if there were an unlit trench on the highway and a man falls into it at night and breaks his leg, he can sue the person responsible for the trench. On the other hand, if a man is one of many motorists who have to endure delay because the presence of the trench closes one carriageway, he cannot sue.

An old case on public nuisance is **Tarry -v- Ashton** (1874) in which a lamp overhanging the highway had not been properly repaired and fell onto a passer-by causing injury. It was held that the passer-by could sue the owner of the land from which the lamp had fallen.

A modern case on this tort is **Attorney-General -v- Castonia Coaches** (1976) in which residents were awarded damages for noise, fumes and obstruction of access to their properties caused by the parking of the defendant's coaches in the road.

PRIVATE NUISANCE is an unlawful interference with the use and enjoyment of a person's land. The interference may take the form of damage to the land itself, e.g. be encroaching tree roots causing subsidence of buildings on the land, or to things on the land, or personal injury to the occupier, or discomfort or inconvenience to the occupier.

A particular form of private nuisance in interference with rights over land such as rights of way, light, support, drainage etc. Excessive noise, dust, dirt, fumes, vibrations, smoke could amount to a nuisance. The following points should be borne in mind in deciding whether an activity or state of affairs constitutes a nuisance:-

1. The law applies the principle of 'give and take' between neighbours: both are entitled to the occasional bonfire and therefore neither can complain.
2. The standard of comfort, peace and quiet varies from area to area: thus a person who lives in a town centre cannot expect the same degree of peace and quiet as if he lived in the country.
3. The fact that the plaintiff may be an abnormally sensitive person is not material. If the plaintiff has a more sensitive nose or more acute hearing than the average person that is his misfortune, it will not render an activity a nuisance.
4. Malice is not an essential element of the tort, but may be relevant as showing the unreasonableness of the activity in question.

   In **Hollywood Silver Fox Farm -v- Emmett** (1936), a farmer sent his son to fire a 12-bore shot gun near the boundary with his neighbour in order to disrupt the breeding activities of his neighbour's silver foxes. The poor vixen did indeed suffer miscarriages! It was held that the malice of the defendant rendered his otherwise lawful shooting, unlawful.
5. The fact that factories and other businesses are good for the economy and provide employment, i.e. are for the public good, is not a defence if their activities cause serious discomfort.

It is no defence that the plaintiff moved to the nuisance. In **Sturges -v- Bridgmen** (1879) a confectioner made a great deal of noise with heavy pestles and mortars for over twenty years. His neighbour, a doctor, then had a surgery built at the bottom of his garden near to the boundary. The doctor then found that the noise was so great that it interfered with the examination of patients. It was held that the noise did amount to a nuisance and that the fact that the plaintiff doctor had moved to it did not defeat his claim. However, in the modern case of **Miller -v- Jackson** (1977), an injunction to restrain the playing of cricket on fields adjoining the plaintiff's property was refused. The plaintiffs were purchasers from a developer who had erected houses adjoining a field on which cricket had been played for over 70 years. Between the time of their purchase in 1972 and 1976 some twenty cricket balls had been hit into the plaintiff's garden. Nevertheless, the court held that the erection of a house could not turn the innocent, beneficial activity of cricket into a nuisance.

6. Normally an isolated occurrence will not amount to a nuisance. However, the 'isolated occurrence' may result from a continuing source of danger in which case there will be liability, as in **Spicer -v- Smee** (1946) in which the defendant's defective electrical wiring caused a fire which destroyed the plaintiff's bungalow. It was held that the defendant was liable.
7. Nuisance is only actionable on proof of damage, i.e. it is not actionable per se.

   An action may be brought by the occupier of premises. Thus an owner-occupier or a tenant may sue, but not a member of the occupier's household or a mere visitor. There is always the possibility, of course, that such a person would have an action in negligence, depending upon the facts. A landlord may sue where there is permanent damage to the value of his property.

The Person who may be sued

The following persons may be sued:-

(i) **The creator** of the nuisance.

(ii) **An occupier** who knows or should know of the existence of the nuisance.

(iii) **A landlord** who lets premises knowing that a nuisance exists or who authorises or permits his tenant to create a nuisance.

DEFENCES

The following are defences to an action in nuisance:-

1. **Long user or prescription**, i.e. that a right has been acquired to continue the nuisance by virtue of its having been in existence openly and continuously for a period of twenty years or more.

   However, the twenty year period does not begin to run until the activity becomes a nuisance, as is clear from **Sturges -v- Bridgman** above. (The noise caused by the pestles and mortars did not become a nuisance until the doctor built his new surgery.)

2. **Statutory authority**, i.e. that an Act of Parliament authorises the activity, e.g. the running of a railway which would otherwise amount to a nuisance.
3. That the use of the land is **lawful and reasonable**. N.B. however, that it is no defence that the defendant used due care and skill to prevent the activity from being a nuisance.

REMEDIES

These are:-

1. **Damages.**
2. **Injunction.**
3. **Abatement** or **self-help**, e.g. lopping of overhanging branches.

If entry onto the neighbour's land is necessary, notice must be given. The sawn-off branches remain the property of the neighbour.

7.13 THE TORT OF RYLANDS v FLETCHER

This tort takes its name from the case of **Rylands -v- Fletcher** (1868) in which Fletcher had a reservoir constructed on his land by independent contractors in order to supply water power to his mill. There were in fact disused mine shafts situated below the reservoir which, unknown to either Fletcher or the contractors, communicated with Ryland's mines. The result was that the water from the reservoir escaped down the shafts and flooded Ryland's mines. It was held by the House of Lords that the defendant, Fletcher, was strictly liable for the damage, i.e. he was liable even though he was not negligent.

The rule or ratio of the case is summed up in the words of Lord Blackburn: "A person who for his own purposes brings on his lands and collects and keeps there anything likely to do mischief if it escapes, must keep it in at his peril, and, if he does not do so, is prima facie answerable for all the damage which is the natural consequence of its escape."

The following points should be noted:-

1. There must be an actual 'escape' from the defendant's land. Therefore in **Red -v- Lyons and Co Ltd** (1947) the claim of an inspector injured by an explosion inside a munitions factory in which she was carrying out an inspection failed.
2. The defendant is not protected from liability by employing an independent contractor.
3. Liability under this rule is confined to things which are not naturally upon land, e.g. explosives, sewage, electricity stored in large quantity. Thus there would be no liability for water in a lake or things which grow naturally, e.g. thistles. There could, of course, be liability in nuisance for such things, depending on the facts.
4. There must be some damage; the tort is not actionable per se.

Defences

Although the tort is one of **strict liability**, there are the folowing defences:-

1. **Act of God**, e.g. an earth tremor.

2. **Act of the Plaintiff**, i.e. the plaintiff's own interference has caused the escape.
3. **Act of a Third Party**, i.e. of a stranger over whom the defendant had no control. N.B. that the defendant does have control over the acts of his employees and, for the purpose of this tort, over his independent contractors. The defendant will not, of course, escape liability if he should have anticipated the act of the third party and guarded against it.
4. **Consent** of the Plaintiff to the presence of the thing which causes the mischief. Common benefit will be evidence of consent to the risk, as in **Peter -v- Prince of Wales Theatres (Birmingham) Ltd** (1943) in which an escape of water from a sprinkler system caused damage to the plaintiff's stock. His claim failed as the sprinkler system benefited both his shop and the part of the building occupied by the defendants as a theatre.
5. **Statutory authority.** This will, of course, depend upon the exact wording of the Statute.

7.14 DEFAMATION

Defamation is an injury to **reputation**. It lowers the person defamed in the eyes of right-thinking members of society by exposing him to hatred, ridicule or contempt, or by prejudicing him in his office, profession or trade, or by causing him to be shunned. The defamatory statement can take the form of written or spoken words or a picture or sculpture. Mere vulgar abuse or insults do not amount to defamation.

Words may be defamatory in their ordinary meaning, e.g. 'he is a liar', or by virtue of an **innuendo**. It is for the plaintiff to prove the innuendo, i.e. to prove that an apparently innocent statement was, by virtue of the circumstances in which is was made, defamatory. It is apparently innocent to state that a man and a woman are engaged to be married; however, the statement will have serious implication if the man is already married to another lady, **Cassidy-v-Daily Mirror Newspapers Ltd** (1929).

The defamatory statement will be **slander if it is in transient form** and **libel if it is in permanent form**. The spoken word is therefore slander. However, it is libel if it is broadcast by radio or television under S.1 **Defamation Act 1952** or is uttered in the course of a play under the **Theatres Act 1968**.

Libel, if it tends to cause a breach of the peace, is a crime; slander is not a crime.

Libel is actionable per se, i.e. without the plaintiff proving damage; **slander is only actionable on proof of damage**, save in the following cases:

1. The defamation consists of a statement that the plaintiff has committed a crime punishable by imprisonment.
2. The defamation consists of a statement that the plaintiff is suffering from an infectious or contagious disease such that others are likely to avoid him.
3. The defamation consists of a statement that a woman plaintiff is guilty of unchastity or adultery.

4. The defamation consists of a statement that is injurious to the plaintiff in respect of any trade, calling, office or profession carried on by him at the time of publication.

In order to succeed in an action for defamation, the plaintiff must prove:-

1. That the defendant's statement was **defamatory**.
2. That the **statement was published**, i.e. made to some third person. There is no publication if the defendant makes a defamatory statement to his own spouse, as statements between spouses are absolutely privileged. The defendant will be liable if he could have foreseen publication even if he did not intend it. Thus in **Theaker -v- Richardson** (1962) the defendant was held liable when a defamatory letter addressed to the plaintiff was opened and read by the plaintiff's husband. However, in **Huth -v- Huth** (1915), the defendant was not liable where a butler opened and read an unsealed defamatory letter addressed to his master. It should be noted that there is a presumption that a postcard is read by those who handle it. The dictation of a defamatory letter to a secretary would also amount to publication, but the occasion may be privileged. Finally, it should be noted that each repetition of a defamatory statement is a fresh publication and gives rise to liability. Thus publishers and printers are liable as well as authors.
3. That the statement **referred to him**, i.e. that people who know him would understand the statement as referring to him. If a writer uses what he believes to be a fictional name for a character in his work, and there is a real person of that name to whom the defamatory statement could refer, then the writer will be liable, as in **Hulton -v- Jones** (1910). Similarly, in **Newstead -v- London Express Newspaper Ltd** (1940), there was a statement that a certain person living in Camberwell had been convicted of bigamy. Unfortunately, there was another man of the same name and he successfully sued for damages. A class of persons cannot be defamed.
4. That **damage** resulted from the defamation, save where the defamation is actionable per se.

Defences

There are the following defences to an action for defamation:-

1. **Truth or justification.** Quite simply, if the statement is true, there is no liability. Moreover, the defence will succeed if the statement is substantially true. Thus the defence would not fail if the defendant had said that the plaintiff had spent ten years in prison, whereas in fact he had only served nine years. The discrepancy would be an immaterial detail: it could not worsen the plaintiff's reputation.
2. **Fair Comment.** The defendant will only succeed with this defence if he can show that he made a comment, i.e. expressed an opinion, on a matter of public interest and that he was not malicious. It is this defence which enables journalists to comment on the utterances and conduct of holders of public office. Similarly, it enables critics to criticise the works of authors.

However, the defence does not licence criticism of the private lives of authors and artists.

3. **Privilege.** This may be either **absolute** or **qualified**. The difference is that malice cannot destroy absolute privilege, but it will destroy qualified privilege.

   Statements are **absolutely privileged** when made in the following circumstances:-

   (i) In the course of judicial proceedings.
   (ii) By a member in either House of Parliament.
   (iii) Between officers of State in the course of their duty.
   (iv) Between officials of the European Communities in the course of their duty.
   (v) By authority of either House of Parliament, e.g. 'Hansard'.
   (vi) In fair, accurate and contemporaneous reports in newspapers of judicial proceedings in the United Kingdom. However, the defence will not apply if they contain blasphemous or indecent material.

   Statements enjoy **qualified privilege** when they are made in the following circumstances:-

   (i) Where there is reciprocal interest or duty in the making and receiving of the statement, e.g. where an employer gives a reference about an employee to a prospective employer.
   (ii) In communications between solicitor and client.
   (iii) In reports of judicial proceedings or proceedings of either House of Parliament provided that such reports are fair and accurate, but they need not be contemporaneous.
   (iv) In reports of foreign judicial proceedings.
   (v) In reports of public meetings or local authority meetings in newspapers.
   (vi) By a person in order to defend himself against an attack on his reputation.

   Thus the effect of qualified privilege is to give immunity, to a person who makes a defamatory statement, but honestly believes in its truth and is not acting from an improper motive. Absolute privilege, by contrast, confers complete immunity even though the maker of the statement may be acting from pure malice.

4. Section 4 of the **Defamation Act 1952** gives a publisher of words which were not intended to be defamatory an opportunity to make amends. The section applies where the publisher published the words innocently and without negligence. The defendant can offer to publish a correction and apology and take reasonable steps to notify persons who received copies of the defamatory matter. In this way, the defendant can protect himself against liability for damages, but a court could order him to pay costs.

The remedies for defamation are damages and, in some circumstances an injunction to prevent a repetition. Exemplary damages may be awarded where the publisher of a defamatory statement stands to make a profit by it.

7.15 **MALICIOUS FALSEHOOD**

This is a false statement made in order to damage a business interest (as opposed to reputation), e.g. a statement that manufacturer X produces goods of poor quality (Slander of Goods), or that he can only sell them cheaply because he is evading payment of tax (Slander of Title).

7.16 **GENERAL PRINCIPLES OF TORTIOUS LIABILITY**

From the above outline of separate torts, it should be apparent that malice is not an essential element of tortious liability. The absence of malice will not render an unlawful action lawful; the presence of malice will not make a lawful action unlawful. In **Bradford Corporation -v- Pickles** (1985), Mr. Pickles wanted to sell some of his land to the Corporation for too high a price. They refused to buy and he retaliated by abstracting water on his own land so as to reduce the amount of water entering the Corporation's reservoir. It was held that his action was lawful and his malicious motive did not render it unlawful. There are, of course, exceptional cases where malice is relevant, e.g. where it is of the essence of the particular tort, e.g. malicious prosecution or malicious falsehood; or in private nuisance, as in **Hollywood Silver Fox Farm -v- Emmett**; or in defamation where it can destroy the defence of qualified privilege.

7.17 **GENERAL DEFENCES**

These are as follows:-

1. **Contributory negligence.** This does not offer a complete defence, but, as we have seen under the heading 'Negligence', has the effect of reducing the plaintiff's damages.
2. **Volenti non fit injuria** (he who consents to run the risk cannot afterwards complain). This defence is of general application, but has been discussed under the heading 'Negligence'.
3. **Self-Defence.** Reasonable force may be used in defending oneself and one's own family, and possibly anybody, against a physical assault (battery). Reasonable force may also be used in defence of property, e.g. in ejecting a trespasser. The force used must be proportionate to the circumstances.
4. **Act of God.** This is some occurrence which could not be foreseen, i.e. the result of natural forces such as an earthquake.
5. **Inevitable Accident.** This is an occurrence without intention or negligence on the part of the defendant. In **Stanley -v- Powell** (1891) the defendant shot at a pheasant, but a pellet ricocheted from a tree and struck the plaintiff. It was held that the defence of inevitable accident succeeded.
6. **Necessity.** This is a defence that the defendant was forced to act as he did because of an emergency, e.g. he had to trespass onto the plaintiff's land in order to prevent the spread of fire to neighbouring land.
7. **Mistake.** Mistake of law is never a defence. Mistake of fact is not normally a defence, but exceptionally, it can be, e.g. it is a defence to the tort of

malicious prosecution that the defendant had a reasonable, though mistaken, belief that the plaintiff was guilty.

8. **Statutory Authority.** The authority of an Act of Parliament may be absolute, i.e. it may authorise an activity regardless of the harm which results from it. On the other hand, the authority may be conditional, i.e. the Act authorises an activity provided that no harm results from it. It is necessary in each instance to examine the exact wording of the Act.

7.18 PARTIES

Any person of full capacity can sue or be sued in tort. The following special cases should be noted:-

1. **Unborn Children.** Under the **Congenital Disabilities (Civil Liability) Act 1976**, a child may sue, once he has been born, for any injury inflicted upon him before his birth. The exception is that he may not sue his own mother, save where he is injured by her negligent driving, as in this case it will be his mother's insurers who will pay the damages.
2. **Minors.** A minor may sue by his 'next friend', e.g. parent or guardian ad litem. However, a minor may not be sued where this would be an indirect means of enforcing a contract on which he is not liable. Parents are not vicariously liable for their children's torts, but they may be liable where they have been personally negligent, i.e. by failing to act as prudent parents.
3. **Spouses.** Under the **Law Reform (Husband and Wife) Act 1962** a husband may sue a wife, and vice versa, save that the court may stay the action where no substantial benefit will accrue to either party from the continuation of the proceedings. Clearly, if one spouse is injured by the other's negligent driving, he, or she, can sue, as the real defendant is the insurance company.
4. **Persons suffering from mental disorder.** The rules are similar to those relating to minors. In particular, the mentally ill, like young children, may be incapable of having the necessary mental state for the tort in question, e.g. the carelessness required for negligence, or the malice required for malicious falsehood.
5. **Diplomats. Foreign Heads of State**, Ambassadors and their staffs cannot be sued by reason of the diplomatic immunity which they enjoy.
6. **The Crown.** By virtue of the **Crown Proceedings Act 1947**, the Crown is liable in the same way as any person of full age and capacity for the torts of its servants or agents. However, a judgment cannot be enforced against the Crown. H.M. The Queen, in her personal capacity cannot be sued.

7.19 JOINT TORTS

Where a tort is committed by two or more persons, they are joint tortfeasors. Their liability to the plaintiff is 'joint and several'. This means that the plaintiff can sue one, some of them, or all of them, for the full damages that he is claiming. The tortfeasor who has had to pay, or the tortfeasors who have had to pay, can then claim a contribution from the other tortfeasors by virtue of the **Law Reform (Married Women and Tortfeasors) Act 1935**. That contribution shall be 'such as may be found by the courts to be just and equitable having regard to the extent of the person's responsibility for the damage in question'.

7.20 VICARIOUS LIABILITY

This means that one person is responsible for the torts committed by another, thus if A can be sued for the torts committed by B, A is vicariously liable for B's torts.

A principal is vicariously liable for the torts committed by his agent, as we have seen in the last chapter. A partner is liable for the torts committed by other partners and, perhaps most importantly of all, an employer is vicariously liable for the torts of his employees committed during the course of their employment. All factors are examined by the courts in deciding whether a person enjoys the status of an employee. The modern approach is to decide whether a person is, or is not, his 'own boss'. If the person is classified as an employee, the employer will be liable for any torts committed by the employee during the course of the latter's employment. Thus the employer will be liable not only for acts which he authorised, but also for an unauthorised way of performing a duty. Only if the tort occurs whilst the employee is on a 'frolic of his own', i.e. outside the scope of the employment will the employer not be liable.

The following cases should be noted:-

1. **Limpus -v- London General Omnibus Co** (1862) in which, contrary to express instructions, a bus driver raced his bus and thereby caused the bus of a rival company to overturn with the result that the plaintiff was injured. It was held that the employers were liable as the driver had merely driven the bus in an unauthorised way. This case should be contrasted with;
2. **Beard -v- London General Omnibus Co** (1900) in which a bus conductor turned the bus at the terminus and injured the plaintiff. It was held that his employers were not liable as he was acting outside the scope of his employment by driving the bus, his duties being confined to conducting the bus.
3. **Rose -v- Plenty** (1976) in which a milkman engaged a boy of thirteen years to help him on his milk-round and injured him by negligent driving of the milk-float. It was held that the employers were liable to the injured boy in spite of the fact that the milkman had defied employers' instructions by engaging the boy.
4. **Lloyd -v- Grace Smith and Co** (1912) in which a managing clerk employed by a firm of solicitors fraudulently induced a widow to convey some cottages to him. It was held that his employers were liable.
5. **Smith -v- Stages** (1989) where the House of Lords stated than an employee travelling on the highway will be acting in the course of his employment if, and only if, he is at the material time going about his employers' business.

A problem can arise, where employer A 'lends' his servant to employer B, as to which employer is responsible for a tort committed by the servant whilst he is 'out on loan'.

In **Mersey Docks and Harbour Board -v- Coggins and Griffiths (Liverpool) Ltd** (1946), a driver was lent with a crane by his employer to another employer. It was held that the first employer remained responsible for the torts of the crane-man as the latter remained responsible to his employer for the safe-keeping of the crane. Such cases will, of course, be decided on their particular facts.

An employer is not normally liable for the acts of an independent contractor, but he will be liable in the following instances:-

(i) where the contractor carries out work on or adjoining the highway, as in **Tarry -v- Ashton** (1876);
(ii) under the rule in **Rylands -v- Fletcher;**
(iii) where the contractor is employed to do an act which is exceptionally dangerous;
(iv) where the employer authorises or ratifies a tortious act.

7.21 LIMITATION

A plaintiff must commence his action in tort within the period laid down by the **Limitation Act 1980** (as amended). If the plaintiff fails to issue his writ or summons within the requisite period, his action is said to be statute-barred. The period runs from the date of accrual of the cause of action, e.g. the date of the accident. The principal periods are as follows:-

(i) three years in the case of death or personal injury;
(ii) twelve years in the case of actions relating to ownership of land;
(iii) six years in most other cases.

The Act contains provision for allowing an injured plaintiff to commence an action outside the three year limit where the plaintiff's 'date of knowledge' is later, e.g. it was only possible for him to realise that his injuries were significant or serious at a later date.

The Act confers on the courts a further discretion to extend the basic time limits where it would be equitable to do so.

The Court must weigh the possible prejudice to the plaintiff against the possible prejudice to the defendant.

In the case of persons suffering under a disability, i.e. minors and those suffering from mental disorder, time only runs from the cessation of the disability or death, whichever first occurs. However, time runs against a minor if he is in the custody of a parent, as the parent can bring an action as his 'next friend'.

Survival of Actions

The general rule under the **Law Reform (Miscellaneous Provision) Act 1934** is that a cause of action in tort survives for the benefit of a deceased plaintiff's estate and against the estate of a deceased defendant. The exceptions to the rule are actions for defamation and claims for exemplary damages: these do not survive death.

Dependants of a deceased person can bring a claim under the **Fatal Accidents Act 1976**.

7.22 REMEDIES

The remedies which may be sought in an action in tort are **damages** and/or **injunction** or **specific restitution**.

Damages may be nominal, e.g. £2, in the case of a tort actionable per se, e.g. trespass, where no actual damage has been suffered.

Exceptionally, contemptuous damages may be awarded, i.e. the smallest coinage of the realm, to mark the fact that there has been a technical breach of the plaintiff's rights, but with no merit in the action.

Damages are normally compensatory or substantial, i.e. they compensate the plaintiff for the actual loss sustained. The object of such damages is to place the plaintiff in the same position as he would have been in if he had not suffered the tortious act. All damages in tort are unliquidated, i.e. they are at the discretion of the court. Substantial damages can be divided into **special** damages and **general** damages. Special damages are awarded in respect of matters which can be quantified before the date of the hearing, e.g. loss of earnings already suffered; general damages are awarded in respect of matters which cannot be quantified before the date of the trial, e.g. future loss of earnings, and such intangible matters as pain and suffering.

As mentioned earlier, in relation to negligence, damages will only be awarded in respect of damage which is not too remote a consequence of the tortious act. The modern law derives from the decision of the Judicial Committee of the Privy council in **Overseas Tankship (UK) Ltd -v- Mort's Dock and Engineering Co Ltd** (1961), known as **The Wagon Mound** after the ship involved. The facts were that the defendants negligently allowed a large quantity of oil to escape from The Wagon Mound in Sydney Harbour. The oil reached the plaintiff's wharf where welding operations were taking place. The plaintiff asked whether it was safe to continue welding and was assured that it was, as oil would not ignite when spread on water. A spark from the welding caused the oil to ignite and the plaintiff's wharf was destroyed. It was held, on the scientific evidence of the time, that the fire was not a reasonably foreseeable consequence of the negligent spillage of the oil and therefore the defendants were not liable. Thus the test which is now applied in order to help determine liability in tort is the test of reasonable foreseeability of consequences.

An exception to this general rule is a category of cases known as the 'eggshell skull' cases. A tortfeasor takes his victim as he finds him. This means that if the tortfeasor inflicts injury, through negligence or otherwise, on a person with some abnormality, e.g. a weak heart, brittle bones, or an exceptionally thin skull, he will be liable for the grave consequences which the victim may suffer. The tortfeasor cannot argue that a normal person would have suffered only trivial injury. Thus in **Smith -v- Leach Brain and Co Ltd** (1961), the defendants were held liable for the death of an employee who had suffered a burn on the lip through the carelessness of a fellow employee who had caused a piece of molten zinc to fly out of a galvanizing tank. The burn would not normally have been serious, but the deceased's body was liable to develop cancer. Although the cancer and the death were not a reasonably foreseeable consequence of the burn, liability arose under the 'thin skull' principle.

A defendant will not, of course, be liable for damage which results, not from his tortious act, but from some new cause, i.e. from a novus actus interveniens. Howver, the novus actus must not be such that it should have been foreseen by the defendant. If he should have foreseen it, he will be liable as in **Scott -v- Shepherd** (1773) where the defendant threw a lighted squib in a market place at one person who hit it away towards another person who in turn hit it towards the plaintiff who was injured when it exploded. It was held that the defendant was liable to the plaintiff as the intervening acts were within the mischief created by the defendant; they did not break the chain of causation. A case in which a novus actus broke the chain of causation is **Hogan -v- Bentinck Collieries Ltd** (1949) in which a miner fractured his thumb while at work. He subsequently had it amputated because he received bad advice. It was held that the amputation was a novus actus and therefore his employers were not liable.

Specific restitution is an order for the return of property belonging to the plaintiff. It is an equitable and, therefore, discretionary remedy.

Injunction is, of course, as mentioned earlier, also an equitable remedy. It is particularly appropriate to prevent the continuation of a nuisance.

PAST EXAMINATION QUESTIONS

Questions are grouped under ''topic headings'' as a matter of convenience but it should be remembered that in response to some questions it will be necessary to bring in a number of topic areas. Questions are principally drawn from the C.I.I. examination papers for years 1982 to 1988 inclusive. However the C.I.I.'s pre-1982 specimen paper has also been used as a source as well as selected questions from the nearest equivalent paper of the 1972-1981 period

SOURCE OF LAW

1. What are the sources of English law? Describe briefly: (a) Common law; (b) Statute law.

2. What are the special characteristics of English law compared with other systems?

3. (a) 'Equity is a gloss or supplement which modifies the common law'. Explain.
   (b) What conditions must be fulfilled before a custom will be recognised by the courts as legally binding?

4. (a) Describe the system of judicial precedent in English Law.
   (b) Explain the meaning of (i) ratio decidendi;
   (ii) obiter dicta.

5. What is delegated legislation, why is it necessary and what are its disadvantages?

ENGLISH LEGAL SYSTEM

1. In what types of case do the county courts have judisdiction?

2. (a) Give three examples of administrative tribunals outlining the functions which they perform.
   (b) What are (i) the advantages and (ii) the disadvantages of administrative tribunals compared with ordinary courts?

3. Outline the scope of judisdiction of the three Divisions of the High Court of Justice, including the Divisional Courts

4. Differentiate between a crime and a civil wrong. What are the objectives of criminal punishments and civil remedies respectively?

5. Explain the nature of a crime. How does a crime differ from a tort?

THE JUDICIARY AND LEGAL PROFESSION

1. What do you understand by the phrase ''independence of the judiciary''? How far do you consider that it exists in England today and by what means is it achieved?

2. What do you consider are the outstanding features of the organisation of the legal profession in England? What merits or demerits do you consider these features possess?

3. Write brief notes on the following:
   (a) the Lord Chancellor;
   (b) Magistrates;
   (c) Coroners
   (d) the Attorney-General

4. To what extent are juries now used in (a) civil and (b) criminal, trials? What are the respective functions of judges and juries?

LEGAL STATUS AND PERSONALITY

1. To what extent is the Crown liable in civil law? In what ways does it differ from other litigants?

2. In what respects are minors treated differently from adults in:
   (a) criminal law
   (b) the law of contract
   (c) the law of torts

3. (a) In what ways does a limited company differ from a partnership?
   (b) What are the main effects of incorporation for a company?

4. Distinguish between corporations sole and corporations aggregate. In what different ways may corporations aggregate be formed?

LAW OF CONTRACT

1. Distinguish between an offer and an invitation to treat. What is the importance of the distinction?

2. What are the main rules that a court will follow in deciding whether a sum, mentioned in a contract, is liquidated damages or a penalty?

3. Distinguish between a condition and a warranty and indicate the legal remedies available for breach of each one.

4. (a) ''Consideration is an essential requirement of a valid contract''. Discuss.
   (b) Under what circumstances will payment of a smaller amount discharge a debt of a greater amount?

5. On what basis does a court proceed to assess damages for breach of contract?

6. What are the principal ways in which a contract can be discharged? Comment briefly on each, illustrating your answer by reference to decided cases.

7. (a) When will payment of a smaller sum discharge a greater debt?
   (b) Christine owes Pam £1000. Christine sends Pam a cheque for £750 with a letter saying 'I am enclosing all the money I have. Please accept this in full satisfaction of my debt'. Pam replies aying 'I accept your cheque for £750 in full satisfaction of your debt'. Two weeks later Pam writes another letter to Chrstine requesting the balance of £250.

   Advise Christine.

LAW OF AGENCY

1. Describe in detail the methods by which an agency can be:
   (a) created
   (b) terminated

2. (a) What do you understand by the term ''agent'' in the legal sense?
   (b) What are the main duties of an agent?

3. Define: (a) express authority
   (b) implied authority
   (c) usual authority
   (d) apparent authority

LAW OF TORTS

1. Define the nature and extent of the defence of 'volenti non fit injuria'.

2. Explain the main provisions of the Limitation Act 1980 as far as they relate to actions in tort.

3. What is meant by the term 'vicarious liability'? In what situation does it arise?

4. (a) Define what is meant by defamation
   (b) What are the main differences between libel and slander?

5. (a) What must be proved in order for a plaintiff to succeed in the tort of negligence?
   (b) What is meant by 'res ipsa loquitur'?

6. MacDonald is building some houses on a plot of land. The building site is surrounded by a high fence and there is a large notice warning unauthorised persons to keep out.

Charles, whilst delivering bricks on the site, trips over some bags of cement and breaks his leg.

That night, after MacDonald has finished work for the day, Edward aged 10, climbs over the fence and falls into an unprotected trench breaking his arm.

Discuss MacDonald's liability in civil law to Charles and to Edward.

CII examination report 1988 020

This report, prepared by the CII's examiners, is intended to help students and teachers in preparing for the examinations by giving an indication of the points which should have been brought out in answers and also examiner's comments on how candidates actually performed in the examinations.

The report shows the main points or headings which examiners were seeking in answer to each question (candidates would be expected to expand upon these points). These are not model answers and should not be regarded as such. There may not indeed be any right or wrong answer to some of the questions, so in cases where candidates displayed imagination and originality, examiners gave them credit even though the answers were not along the lines expected.

Great care is taken in the setting of all papers. For each subject there is a senior examiner who is required to present the paper he has set to a panel of experts and an assessor. Each paper is carefully scrutinised to ensure that there are no ambiguities, errors or inconsistencies and that the paper is generally fair. Assessors and examiners are carefully selected from the insurance industry for their technical expertise and experience and they must be sympathetic to the educational philosophy of the Institute and the needs of the students. The Institute cannot enter into any correspondence about the suggested main points for the answers.

CII Tuition Service study courses include a copy of the latest report. Other 1988 reports can also be obtained separately and most of the 1987 reports are still available; the cost is £1.10 a copy.

ARRANGEMENT

All matter reproduced from the question paper itself is enclosed in boxes. The examiners' comments appear in italic type. First there is a general comment upon candidates' overall performance. Each question is then treated separately: the question itself is printed in a box, then a brief statement of the points that the examiners expected candidates to deal with in their answers, and finally, in italic type, the examiners' comments on how well candidates answered that particular question in the examination.

020 English Law

Three hours are allowed for this paper. Answer SIX questions only. All questions carry equal marks.

The general standard of this paper was an improvement on last year's with a higher proportion of candidates giving more satisfactory answers. This year was unusual in that, in general, candidates performed better in the 'bookwork' questions than the 'problem' questions. This is disappointing because learning the law is only the first step; applying it to problems is the real test of a candidate's ability.

QUESTION 1

(a) Whilst at a party, Terry agrees to buy Arthur's car for £500. He hands over £500 to Arthur and takes immediate delivery of the car. Arthur now claims that he was drunk when the sale was agreed and informs Terry that he intends suing him for the return of the car. What is the legal position?

(b) What types of contracts are binding on a minor?

(a) A contract made by a drunken person is binding on him if it is for necessaries.

All other contracts are voidable, but only if at the time of the making of the contract the other party to it was aware of the drunkenness.

As the contract is not one for the supply of necessaries, Arthur can only repudiate the contract if he can show Terry was aware that Arthur was drunk and therefore incapable of realising the effect of what he was doing.

Arthur must, in addition, repudiate within a reasonable time of becoming sober.

(b) A minor is a person under the age of eighteen - Family Law Reform Act, 1969.
The following contracts are binding:
- contracts for the supply of necessaries which have been delivered,
- contracts of education and service,
- contracts of marriage, with consent of parent, guardian or the court as appropriate.

Part (a) produced some very poor answers. Many candidates only considered drunkenness as a defence to crimes and those who considered its relevance to the law of contract failed to point out that if the car was not a necessary, the contract is valid unless Terry was

aware of Arthur's drunkenness. Part (b) was generally well answered although some candidates obtained no marks because they only gave those contracts which are NOT binding on minors.

QUESTION 2

MacDonald is building some houses on a plot of land. The building site is surrounded by a high fence and there is a large notice warning unauthorised persons to keep out.

Charles, whilst delivering bricks on the site, trips over some bags of cement and breaks his leg.

That night, after MacDonald has finished work for the day, Edward aged 10, climbs over the fence and falls into an unprotected trench breaking his arm.

Discuss MacDonald's liability in civil law to Charles and to Edward.

Under the Occupiers' Liability Act, 1957 an occupier of land owes to all visitors a common duty of care. That duty is to 'take such care as in all the circumstances of the case is reasonable to see that the visitor will be reasonably safe in using the premises for the purposes for which he is invited or permitted by the occupier to be there'.

Under the Occupiers' Liability Act, 1984 the occupier owes persons other than visitors (i.e. trespassers) a duty to take such care as is reasonable in all the circumstances to see that the uninvited entrant does not suffer injury on the land by reason of any danger on the land.

Charles is a visitor but MacDonald will only be liable in tort if the bag of cement presented an unreasonable hazard. Presumably visitors to building sites would expect the odd item of building material to be lying around. The duty owed by MacDonald to Edward is lower than that owed to Charles as Edward is a trespasser. Does the unprotected trench constitute a 'danger' of which MacDonald should be aware? Is it reasonable for MacDonald to believe that children will climb into the site? Should MacDonald offer any protection to trespassers? It is unlikely MacDonald will be liable.

This question was undoubtedly the one that produced the worst answers; mainly because the majority of candidates failed to realise that it called for a discussion of occupiers' liability. In many cases candidates briefly mentioned negligence or employers' liability but nothing else and it was also disappointing that many candidates were unaware of the 1984 Act.

QUESTION 3

(a) What relationships give rise to a presumption of undue influence under the law of contract?

(b) George recently joined a religious sect to which he made a gift of £25,000. George has now left the sect following a disagreement and would like to recover the £25,000. What is the legal position?

(a) Undue influence means that one party to the contract enters into it in such circumstances that he cannot be said to be exercising his own free judgment.

The following relationships give rise to a presumption of undue influence due, it is considered, to the unequal bargaining power of the respective parties:
- doctor and patient
- parent and child
- solicitor and client
- religious advisor and member of his congregation
- trustee and beneficiary.

(b) Undue influence makes a contract voidable at the option of the party suffering from it, provided they repudiate the contract within a reasonable time.

In this case, George must prove undue influence and if he does he will be able to recover the £25,000 but only if he brings an action within a reasonable time - **Allcard v Skinner.**

Another poorly answered question. Many candidates who were able to give a tolerably acceptable answer to part (a) completely failed to see the relevance of undue influence in part (b). A major source of confusion was to argue that because George had received no consideration for his gift, he was entitled to recover his money because no contract existed.

QUESTION 4

(a) In what circumstances is the equitable remedy of specific performance available?

(b) Clive, a conjuror, has a long term contract to perform nightly at Mario's night club and nowhere else without Mario's permission. Clive has now been offered a more lucrative contract which he has accepted involving an immediate overseas tour. What remedies are available to Mario?

(a) The equitable remedy of specific performance whereby the court orders the defendant to carry out their part of the contract, is available as a remedy for breach of contract when an award of damages would be inadequate.

A grant of specific performance is always at the discretion of the court.

(b) Clive is in breach of his contract with Mario and Mario can therefore sue for damages.

Mario will not be granted specific performance to compel Clive to carry on working for him as the court cannot superintend performance.

Mario may be granted an injunction preventing Clive taking up the overseas contract - **Lumley v Wagner.**

If Clive can establish that the clause in his contract with Mario preventing him from performing elsewhere without Mario's permission is an unreasonable restraint of trade, the clause will be deemed void and Mario will only be awarded damages for breach of contract.

Part (a) was fairly well answered although many candidates misread the question and gave those circumstances where specific performance was not available. Part (b) was, on the whole, badly answered. The most common cause for loosing marks was to refer only to the possible restraint of trade without considering the more relevant remedies of injunction and specific performance.

QUESTION 5

(a) Distinguish a crime from a civil wrong.

(b) What are the main aims of punishment for a crime?

(a) The purpose of civil proceedings is to enable persons to enforce their rights or to recover their property for their own benefit.

The purpose of criminal proceedings is to enforce law and order in the interests of the community, generally by punishing the offender.

Although in general, a civil offence is a wrong against an individual whereas a criminal offence is a wrong against the community, there are many exceptions and some acts are civil wrongs and also crimes, e.g. assault and battery.

The real distinction is determined by noting the nature of the legal consequences (i.e. proceedings) which follow and whether compensation is awarded or a punishment is imposed.

(b) The aims of punishment for a crime are:
- vengeance; it is necessary to reflect public feelings and prevent personal vengeance;
- deterrence; the objective is to deter a recurrence of the offence by the offender and also to deter others;
- protection of the community; this is the most successful objective;
- reformation; this is the most useful purpose but is generally regarded as unsuccessful.

Easily the most popular question and by far and away the best answered. There were some very good answers indeed to part (a). The only real problem was encountered by those candidates who in part (b) discussed the various forms of punishments.

QUESTION 6

(a) What is arbitration?

(b) Why may people prefer to refer disputes to arbritration rather than to the ordinary courts?

(a) Arbitration is a method of resolving a dispute, for example under an insurance contract, whereby an expert makes an award and the parties do not resort to court proceedings.

Arbitration proceedings are subject to control under the Arbitration Acts 1950-1979 and there is only a right of appeal, which is to the High Court, if a question of law arises out of the award.
It is permissible to exclude rights of appeal on questions of law in certain cases.

(b) The advantages of arbitration are:
- proceedings are comparatively private
- proceedings are less formal
- the dispute is often dealt with more quickly
- it is less expensive than normal litigation
- arbitrators are usually persons well-versed in technicalities of the matters on which they are asked to adjudicate.

In part (a) there was considerable confusion with tribunals in general, and ACAS in particular. Part (b) was well answered.

QUESTION 7

(a) What are the rules of statutory interpretation?

(b) State the conditions that must apply in order for a custom to be legally recognised.

(a) The rules of statutory interpretation are:

(i) The literal rule whereby words and phrases are construed by the courts in their ordinary sense and the ordinary rules of grammar and punctuation are applied.

The rule involves two subsidiary rules:
- the **noscitur a sociis** rule whereby the meaning of a word must be determined by its context;
- the **ejusdem generis** rule whereby the meaning of any general term is dependent on any specific terms which precede it.

(ii) The golden rule enables the courts to assume that Parliament did not intend an absurdity and if the meaning of words in a statute strictly applied would lead to an absurdity, the Act may be construed to avoid the absurdity and give it the meaning which Parliament intended.

(iii) The mischief rule enables the courts to take into account the reasons why the legislation was passed when it is not clear whether an act falls within what is prohibited by a particular piece of legislation. The judge should then adopt a construction that will suppress the mischief and advance the remedy.

(b) The following conditions must apply for a custom to be legally recognised:
- immemorial existence
- continuity
- reasonableness
- certainty
- peaceful user
- compulsion
- not contrary to statute.

Another very popular question which was, on the whole, well answered. Some candidates gave the system of judicial precedent in part (a) but generally those who knew the subject obtained very high marks.

QUESTION 8

Write notes on THREE of the following:

(a) The Lord Chancellor;
(b) The Lord Chief Justice;
(c) The Master of the Rolls;
(d) The Attorney General.

a) The Lord Chancellor is:
- a member of the Cabinet and the Government
- head of the judicial system
- the senior judge of the House of Lords
- appointed by the Crown on the advice of the Prime Minister
- reponsible for the appointment of JPs and advises the Crown on the appointment of High Court Judges.

(b) The Lord Chief Justice is:
- the head of the Court of Appeal - Criminal Division
- appointed by the Crown on the advice of the Prime Minister
- head of the Queen's Bench Division of the High Court
- a barrister of at least 15 years' standing.

(c) The Master of the Rolls:
- is the senior judge of the Court of Appeal - Civil Division
- has supervisory power over solicitors
- is appointed by the Crown on the advice of the Prime Minister.

(d) The Attorney General:
- is a barrister and member of the government but not the Cabinet
- advises the government on matters of law
- conducts civil proceedings, particularly in revenue matters, on behalf of the Crown
- leads for the Crown in important criminal prosecutions
- his consent is required before certain types of proceedings, e.g. under the Official Secrets Act, can be commenced
- can stop a trial on indictment by entering a **'nolle prosequi'**
- supervises the work of the Director of Public Prosecutions
- is leader of the Bar.

This was the least popular question but was reasonably well answered. Candidates did not, in general, give incorrect answers, simply incomplete ones. For example, many contented themselves with simply explaining the Lord Chancellor's legislative role and ignoring his executive and judicial functions or referring to the Master of the Rolls' supervisory role over solicitors and ignoring his judicial position. Exceptionally, the role of the Attorney General was well answered.

TABLE OF STATUTES